# CAREER
# CHANGE
# IS
# CHAOS

# CAREER CHANGE IS CHAOS

## Unless You Find Your Purple Purpose

### Myriem Slater

GRAMMAR
FACTORY
— EST° 2013 —

Published by Grammar Factory Publishing, an imprint of MacMillan
Company Limited.

Grammar Factory Publishing
MacMillan Company Limited
25 Telegram Mews, 39th Floor, Suite 3906
Toronto, Ontario, Canada
M5V 3Z1

www.grammarfactory.com

Slater, Myriem
Career Change Is Chaos: Unless You Find Your Purple Purpose / Myriem
Slater.

Paperback ISBN 978-1-998756-98-8
Hardcover ISBN 978-1-998528-00-4
eBook ISBN 978-1-998756-99-5
Audiobook ISBN 978-1-998528-01-1

1. BUS012000 BUSINESS & ECONOMICS / Careers / General.
2. BUS037020 BUSINESS & ECONOMICS / Careers / Job Hunting.
3. BUS107000 BUSINESS & ECONOMICS / Personal Success.

PRODUCTION CREDITS
Cover design by Designerbility
Interior layout design by Setareh Ashrafologhalai
Book production and editorial services by Grammar Factory Publishing

GRAMMAR FACTORY'S CARBON
NEUTRAL PUBLISHING COMMITMENT
Grammar Factory Publishing is proud to be neutralizing the carbon
footprint of all printed copies of its authors' books printed by or ordered
directly through Grammar Factory or its affiliated companies through the
purchase of Gold Standard-Certified International Offsets.

# Contents

# Introduction

CHANGING CAREERS is as simple as a walk in the park, right? It's all sunshine, rainbows and unicorns—just a simple, stress-free switch from one job to another, no obstacles in sight.

'Transferable skills? Of course, everyone wants a rocket scientist to flip burgers. No problem!'

'Networking? Easy peasy! Just walk up to a stranger and say, "Hi, I have no idea what I'm doing, but can we be friends?"'

'Money matters? Who needs money anyway? It's just a small detail. Let's focus on the joy of being broke.'

'Fear of the unknown? No fear here! I love uncertainty. It's like a box of chocolates: you never know what you're going to get.'

Oh, wait a minute—nobody has ever said any of those things. *Ever.*

Changing careers can feel like jumping off a cliff with a blindfold on: it's scary, it's unknown, and it's risky. But for many people, the thought of staying in a job that doesn't fulfil them is even scarier.

So, essentially, career change is chaos. It's like being stuck on a tightrope over a pool filled with sharks: you're scared to leap and try to swim for safety, but staying put on that jittery wire is even scarier. It's like a saying we have in Morocco, '*wil wil*'—which means the opposite of 'win-win'.

# Acknowledgements

I WOULD LIKE to begin by acknowledging the Traditional Custodians of the land on which I live and work, the Gadigal people of the Eora Nation. I pay my deepest respects to their Elders, past, present and emerging, and recognise their enduring connection to the lands, waters and skies of this beautiful country.

This book was written across three extraordinary locations—Morocco, the Maldives and Australia—but it is Sydney that I call home, and where I have the privilege of residing on the lands of the Gadigal people. I honour their history, their stories and their culture, which continue to enrich the fabric of Australia. May this book, in its small way, contribute to the ongoing journey of learning, healing and respect for the First Nations peoples of this country.

FIRST AND FOREMOST, I wish to express my deepest gratitude to Allah for His countless blessings and for guiding me through life. It is through His infinite mercy that I have been able to reach this point, write this book, and share my wisdom with others.

I also want to express my gratitude to you, the reader, for choosing to embark on this journey with me. Your trust in these words and your desire to grow are truly inspiring. I hope this book serves as a valuable guide in helping you find your path and purpose.

I would also like to express my heartfelt gratitude to my parents, Ali and Alia, for their unwavering support and for raising me with values that have always pushed me to be not only successful but also, and above all, a good person. I am truly blessed to have such incredible parents who have been there for me every step of the way.

To my beloved siblings, Zineb and Youssef, thank you for always standing by my side and believing in me. Your love and support have been a constant source of strength, and I am grateful beyond words for both of you.

Additionally, I would like to honour the memory of Trent Slater, the father of my son. Trent was an exceptional PE teacher, passionate about health and wellbeing, and an amazing teacher who inspired so many. I believe he would have been incredibly proud of me for writing this book and undoubtedly the first to buy a copy. Though he is no longer with us, his values and dedication to living a purposeful life continue to inspire me and others.

And, of course, to my handsome husband, Brett, and our beautiful children, Noah and Sophia. Thank you for the immense joy and love you bring into my life. Every day spent with you inspires me to be better, and I am grateful for the time we share and for your beautiful hearts that light up my world.

With all my love and gratitude,

**MYRIEM SLATER**

But the fact is, when you're stuck in a career that you know in your heart is not for you anymore—or never was in the first place—doing nothing is simply not an option. It's like driving in reverse on the highway of life. Taking action to change your situation, meanwhile, may feel like strapping on a rocket pack and soaring out into the wild blue yonder: as terrifying as it might feel in the moment, it also opens up a whole horizon of possibilities for yourself.

There's no magic potion or secret recipe that will guarantee success. But the fact is, you've already got the power to make it happen. All you need to do is *uncover your purpose.*

Now, what do I mean by 'purpose'?

Purpose is a reason for being. It's a vision of a life that is meaningful, fulfilling and driven by one's passions, values and beliefs. It provides a sense of direction and motivation; it's that guiding light that helps you navigate through life, leading to greater satisfaction and success in both your personal and professional life.

This is why uncovering your purpose is so crucial when it comes to changing careers. Embarking on such a major transition without knowing your purpose is like driving through an unfamiliar landscape without a GPS or a map—desperately searching for landmarks, frantically trying to just get *out* rather than charting a course to an actual destination.

That's where this book comes in. As someone who has undergone a career change, I know the struggles and obstacles one can face on the journey to finding their true calling. That's why I created the Purposeek Coaching Method—to bring together my own insights and knowledge and structure them in a way that will help others find their purpose, and, through that, ultimately achieve their goals. By combining the power of design thinking with my own real-life experiences, the Purposeek Coaching Method provides a roadmap for anyone looking to make a change in their career.

Whether you're just starting out or are in the midst of a transition, this method will support you every step of the way. Now, you may be asking yourself: 'How does this book stand apart from the rest? What does the Purposeek Coaching Method offer that other coaching strategies don't?'

- **Holistic**—the Purposeek Coaching Method considers aspects of both your life and your career as a whole, ensuring a balanced and integrated approach to personal and professional growth.

- **Innovative**—the Purposeek Coaching Method is uniquely designed, drawing on approaches and techniques from the business world to serve personal development.

- **Proven**—the Purposeek Coaching Method has helped many people make positive change in their lives and careers.

In the nearly four years since I founded Purposeek Coaching, I've had the privilege of working with hundreds of professionals from diverse industries, specialisations and backgrounds through my intensive five-week coaching program and personalised one-on-one sessions. The feedback has been overwhelmingly positive, with many participants sharing how the Purposeek Coaching Method has provided them with a clear direction and, in numerous cases, led them directly to successful new careers. Of those who have attended the program:

- **95%** have completed the entire five-week course,

- **98%** recommend the Purposeek Coaching program,

- **90%** report a significant increase in confidence levels after completing the program, and

- **75%** have found their mission and started a new career aligned with their purpose.

These numbers reflect the transformative power of the Purposeek Coaching program and the lasting impact it has had on participants' lives and careers.

The one regret I have about the Purposeek Coaching program is that I can't work with as many people as I would like—not least because, as my career-change journey involved founding and running three other businesses as well, I simply don't have the time! That's why I was inspired to write this book: to take the techniques and strategies that I've personally seen have such a profound effect on so many people's lives, and share them with as wide an audience as possible.

You may have been wondering, when you first picked up this book, what that rather curious combination of words on the cover was referring to: 'Purple Purpose'. While it might sound a little cute, the concept it's describing embodies the core philosophy of this book.

As the first part of the title says, career change can indeed be chaotic; filled with uncertainty, fear and doubt. This often stems from a lack of direction and clarity, which accompanies the monumental task of redefining one's professional life. It's a time of tough decisions and emotional turmoil. But here's the silver lining: it doesn't have to be this way.

This is where your Purple Purpose comes into play. The colour purple, a blend of red's energy and blue's calm, symbolises the balance between action and reflection necessary for true fulfilment. When you find your Purple Purpose, that chaos begins to make sense. Your Purple Purpose is the vibrant, powerful force that drives you forward, turning chaos into a meaningful, purpose-driven journey. It's a beacon that constantly reminds you that your career-change journey should be as unique as you are—that it's not about simply bouncing around from one job to another in an unfocused search for fulfilment, but about finding a role that resonates deeply with your core values and aspirations.

In the chapters that follow, I will ask you to work through the introspective activities and collaborative exercises I share with you so that you can start to define your own Purple Purpose, and then put what you learn into action. By the time you finish this book, you'll be equipped with the tools and insights you need to unleash your full potential, and make the change you need in order to live a happy and fulfilled life.

And the great news is, as daunting as that journey might seem at the outset, the first step is easy. Just turn the page!

# Chapter 1

# Introducing the Purposeek Coaching Method

BEFORE I INTRODUCE you to the foundational principles of the Purposeek Coaching Method, I want to introduce myself—not because I want to hog the spotlight, but because my own career-change journey informed and helped shape the method I was later able to share with other people.

So, let me just lay out the broad strokes. I'm a former finance director and finance consultant, and have worked with such firms as Accenture, Deloitte and EY. A little over three years ago, I left all that behind to become an entrepreneur and multi-business owner, as well as a life and career coach.

Why did I decide to take that leap into the unknown, after nearly two decades—as well as a good deal of success—in the corporate world? See if the below sounds at all familiar to you.

Do you ever feel like work is just a necessary evil to pay the bills and support your family? I used to feel that way too. I dreaded Monday mornings, and couldn't wait for Friday afternoons and holidays. I had a whole host of excuses that would automatically pop into my mind to try to balance out what I was feeling: 'I have a fancy title', 'I have a comfortable lifestyle', and (perhaps the most persuasive one) 'I need to support my family'. But no matter how often I rehearsed those justifications, I was stressed, anxious, unhappy, and on the brink of burnout.

And then, I had an epiphany: Why should any of us accept living like that, and for so long?

So, I took a step back, and began to reflect on how I'd wound up in my career to begin with. Years earlier, when I was growing up in Morocco, I had been a young and ambitious student with a burning desire to succeed. I studied hard, landed a spot at a prestigious business school in France, and chose finance as a career through a combination of family pressure, visa issues, and the recommendation of a professor who advised that specialisation so that I could find a job straight after I finished my studies.

And that's exactly what I did. I worked hard, climbed the corporate ladder, and made it to the role of finance director. But, thinking back on that time during my moment of crisis, I realised that even way back then, at what should have been the exciting first flush of success, I had felt like something was missing.

Some of that feeling was compensated for by an enormous amount of fulfilment on the personal side, as, after I'd moved to Australia to improve my English, I happened to meet a handsome Aussie man and started a family. But as I continued working in my field, I was constantly asking myself, 'Is this my true career path? What else could I be doing? Is this all there is to life?'

At that crossroads moment three years ago, I realised that I had been so focused on the 'what' and 'how' of my career that I had completely ignored the 'why'. I had been living for others, and for a goal that wasn't truly my own. I had never truly taken the time to reflect on my true passions, my true values—my Purple Purpose. But now, I knew that I absolutely had to take that leap of faith and make a break with the career I'd known to that point.

The problem was, even though I was ready for a career change, I didn't know where to start. With the skills that I had built in the consulting industry, there were so many options I could consider—which was a problem in itself, as having so many options can be overwhelming! Should I stay in the corporate world, but in a different role? Should I start my own business? Should I go back to school and learn new skills?

I didn't know. And, as I delved deeper into my thoughts, I felt like a ship lost at sea. The more I tried to confront my fears, the more they consumed me. But I knew there had to be a way out of this spiral of confusion and hopelessness; I just had to keep searching for it. As Victor Hugo once wrote, 'Even the darkest night will end and the sun will rise.'

And let me assure you, it did rise. I took a career break (which was also a brain break), and used that time to start the journey of introspection that eventually led me to my Purple Purpose. And, with that as my guide, I was able to make the change I needed to put myself on the career path I now knew I had always wanted—one aspect of which, of course, is helping others to find their own unique purpose as well, through the Purposeek Coaching Method.

## The Purposeek Coaching Method: The Foundation

The foundation of the Purposeek Coaching Method is *self-empowerment*—which, simply put, means moving from 'I should' to 'I *will*'. I believe that everyone has the power to make their life what they want it to be, and that by focusing on your strengths, values, talents and past experiences you can uncover your purpose and create a clear vision for your future. The goal of the Purposeek Coaching Method is to help you unleash that power by guiding and motivating you to start following your own unique path.

The journey to self-empowerment can be challenging, but I have designed the Purposeek Coaching Method to support you every step of the way by providing you with the tools and resources you need to overcome obstacles and stay on track. Whether you're looking to achieve a specific goal or just want to improve your overall well-being in your work, it will help you make it happen.

## The Purposeek Coaching Method: The Pillars

If self-empowerment is the foundation of the Purposeek Coaching Method, its two pillars are *introspection* and *collaboration*—one inner-directed, the other outer-directed. And it is by locating the right intersection of these two forces that you will be able to discover your true purpose.

Take a look at the diagram below, which I call the Purpose Model.

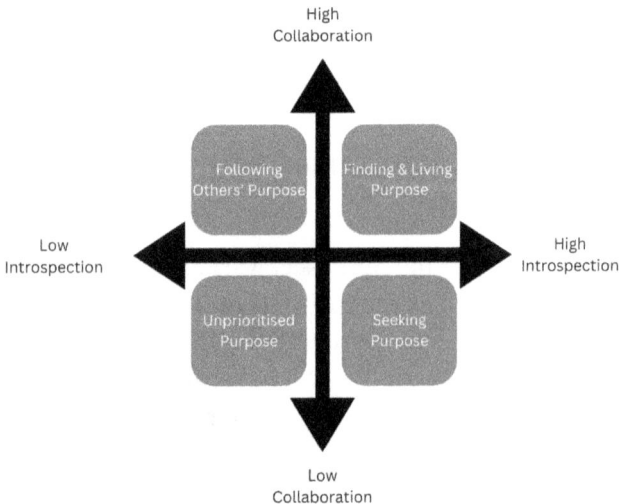

High
Collaboration

Following
Others' Purpose

Finding & Living
Purpose

Low
Introspection

High
Introspection

Unprioritised
Purpose

Seeking
Purpose

Low
Collaboration

As you can see from the diagram, you will get different results by combining different levels of introspection and collaboration. For example, at the very bottom of the scale in the lower-left quadrant is the combination of low introspection and low collaboration. This will yield minimal progress and clarity, as you are neither reflecting on your true self nor engaging with others to gain new perspectives. This means that you are not prioritising your purpose, which leads to stagnation and a lack of direction.

If you do a lot of introspection but not enough collaboration (lower-right quadrant), you may be doing very well in terms of *seeking* your purpose but not so well in terms of *finding* it. When you are constantly in your head, overthinking and not sharing or doing anything about your thoughts or your self-discovery, it can feel like you're wasting your time and clouding your vision instead of clarifying it.

Conversely, as you can see in the top-left quadrant, if you do a lot of collaboration but not enough introspection, you can find yourself living others' purpose rather than your own, as you will not know what really matters to *you*. This can result in losing your sense of self and perpetually living in the shadow of others, dimming your inner light and leading to feelings of dissatisfaction and a lack of fulfilment.

If I were given a choice between feeling lost or living someone else's purpose, I would pick neither. So, as you can see, your only suitable option is to combine your introspective and collaborative activities in a balanced way in order to find your purpose and your true career path. But how do you find that balance?

Glad you asked!

## The Purposeek Coaching Method: The Four Key Principles

This is where the Four Ps of the Purposeek Coaching Method come in: *Purpose, Perspective, Prosperity* and *Plan.*

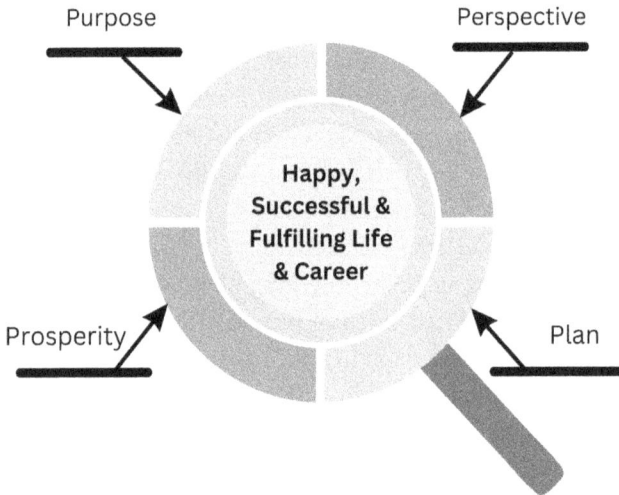

**Purpose** is the foundation of a fulfilling career. What do you want to achieve in your life and what are your passions? To determine your purpose, you need to reflect on what truly makes you happy and what you're naturally good at. This self-awareness will help you find a career that aligns with your values and passions.

**Perspective** is all about looking at things from a different angle. This can mean changing your mindset, seeking new experiences and learning from others. Being open to new ideas and new ways of doing things can help you identify previously unexpected career opportunities and fresh, innovative means of achieving your goals.

**Prosperity** means manifesting the success and abundance you desire. It encourages you to focus on both your material and emotional well-being, ensuring that your career change leads to a holistic and rewarding success. By setting clear intentions and aligning your actions with your values, you can attract prosperity into your life.

**Plan** is the final key to your success. Once you've found your purpose, changed your perspective and started manifesting your prosperity, it's time to take action through such things as researching new career paths, networking, and/or developing new skills that will bring you closer to your career-change goal. Your plan should be realistic and achievable, with specific steps and deadlines.

As we move through this book, you'll see in greater detail how each one of these principles will be brought to bear as you progress on your career-change journey. But let's take a little bit of action right now to get you started on engaging with and absorbing these crucial concepts.

In the space provided below, jot down what response each of these four statements evokes in you. Above all, *be candid* in your answers. If you find one or more of these concepts intriguing, try to explain why. If you think one or more of them is just a cliché or a bit of fluffy, life-coaching nonsense, state your reasons.

- Finding your **Purpose**

- Changing your **Perspective**

- Manifesting your **Prosperity**

- Actioning your **Plan**

Whatever your initial reactions are, they will tell you something about why you picked up this book in the first place, and what your mindset is as we embark on this journey together.

So if you're hesitant or sceptical at this point, don't worry! As you'll soon see, the whole point of the Purposeek Coaching Method is not only to inspire you to find your true purpose, but to provide you with some of the tools and strategies you'll need to make it happen.

## The Four Ps in practice: The plan of this book

The Four Ps of the Purposeek Coaching Method provide the underlying structure for everything in this book.

The largest section of the book (Chapters 2 to 7) are all directed towards the first and most important P—'Purpose'. We will start by exploring the concept of career change itself, setting the stage for a deep dive into understanding who you really are at your core. In Chapters 3 and 4 we will work to create a 'mind map' that will help you visualise your key values, passions, desires and needs, which I refer to as your *four explorers*. This will be further developed in Chapter 5, where we will delve into your intrinsic motivations (or what I call your *drivers*). Chapters 6 and 7 will then discuss how you can channel those motivations into a state of '*flow*', while also navigating around the *external factors* that could negatively impact your journey.

The 'Purpose' section of the book reaches its climax in Chapter 8, where you will draw on all the constructive work you've completed in the previous chapters to create your own *purpose statement*, a powerful and concrete expression of your vision and intent for your career-change journey.

With this crystallised understanding of your Purpose in hand, the next two chapters will expand on it through exercises that draw on the next two Ps, 'Perspective' and 'Prosperity'. In Chapter 9, we will work to identify your top three potential career paths, and then single out the one that best aligns with your Purpose. Then, in Chapter 10, you'll learn about techniques that can help equip you with the right mental framework to reach your goals, showing you how you can overcome your fears, build resilience, and develop a *growth mindset* (which is the very definition of 'manifesting your Prosperity').

The last two chapters bring us to the fourth P, 'Plan'. In Chapter 11 you will learn how to *take action* by breaking down your goals into manageable tasks, so that you can create a roadmap for your career-change journey that will ensure you stay on course. Finally, Chapter 12 will focus on how you can build *sustainable habits* that will help you maintain your momentum over the long term.

So now, without further ado—let's set off on the voyage of self-discovery that will lead you to your very own Purple Purpose, and the genuinely rewarding and fulfilling career you've always dreamed of!

# Chapter 2

# Exploring the Concept of Career Change

THE FIRST STEP in your career-change journey is to understand what career change truly means to *you*. Career change isn't just about switching jobs or industries—it's a multifaceted process that involves self-realisation, exploration, and a willingness to embrace new possibilities.

In this chapter, we'll first explore the reasons why you might want to change careers. Then, we will debunk some of the common misconceptions that often hold people back from pursuing their career dreams. Finally, we'll do some exercises that will help you clearly envision what your ideal career path could be, and how it aligns with your goals and values.

## What are you looking for in a career change?

Before you start updating your resume, filling out job applications or daydreaming about how you can create the next big unicorn start-up, you need to take a step back and ask yourself a crucial question: 'What the heck am I actually looking for in a career change, anyway?'

It's important to reflect on what you truly want and need from your next career move so that you can begin laying the groundwork for getting there. Is it a better work–life balance? More opportunities for growth? A chance to pursue a passion? Whatever your driving motive, by taking the time to get clear on your goals and priorities you can make a more informed decision and increase your chances of finding a career that truly fits you.

### i. Finding your place on the Career Change Spectrum
People approach the prospect of career change from all kinds of different angles. Some view it as a challenging and stressful process, associated with leaving one's comfort zone and taking perhaps unwelcome risks. Others may see it as a means to seek greater fulfilment and/or financial stability, or a response to job loss or dissatisfaction with their current career path. It can also be viewed as a positive opportunity for personal and professional growth, offering a chance to explore new interests and gain new experiences.

Look at the diagram of the Career Change Spectrum below, and circle the motivation that best applies to you.

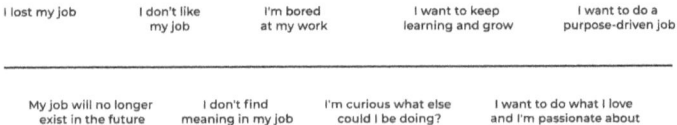

| I lost my job | I don't like my job | I'm bored at my work | I want to keep learning and grow | I want to do a purpose-driven job |
|---|---|---|---|---|

| My job will no longer exist in the future | I don't find meaning in my job | I'm curious what else could I be doing? | I want to do what I love and I'm passionate about |
|---|---|---|---|

If you don't feel that any of the statements above are applicable to your situation, use the space below to write down your motivation. Then, add it to the Career Change Spectrum above at the spot where you think it would be most accurately positioned.

Understanding where you fall on the Career Change Spectrum is the key first step in determining what kind of career change will bring you the most satisfaction and success. For example, if you've lost your job, you may be more likely to have to take a bold, daring move in order to stay afloat in the job market. On the other hand, if you're simply bored in your current role and looking for new opportunities, you may be able to take more calculated risks as you explore uncharted waters.

## ii. Delving into your motivations for career change

Now that you've identified your position on the Career Change Spectrum, you need to understand the driving forces behind your decision so that you can properly tailor the strategies and approach you'll need to take in your search. Knowing your primary motivations will help you fashion the compass that will guide you through your career-change journey.

Grab your pen and jot down the reasons you want to make a change. What are you looking for in this new career path? I won't provide examples, because every career-change journey is unique.

### iii. Why do you want to quit your current job?

Career change often entails leaving your current job. The reasons for that departure often boil down to two situations:

- You want to quit your job because you hate it, or

- You want to quit your job because you've grown too comfortable in it.

A quick note here that the kind of career change you're contemplating at the moment may not involve quitting your job at all, but simply exploring other options within it. However, even if that is the case, I still advise you to read the following sections on these two situations, as they are at the root of so many people's decisions to change their career trajectories—and, sad to say, you might eventually find yourself in one of them even if you're not there right now.

Situation 1: 'I want to quit my job because I hate it.'

There are all kinds of reasons that people feel like they hate their jobs. Perhaps the work you're doing doesn't align with your passions and values, or maybe there's not enough room for growth and development. Alternatively, it could be an unhealthy work–life balance, or simply a long commute. Whatever the case, once you identify the root cause of your discomfort with your current job, you can start to explore potential solutions.

Below, write down the main reason(s) you feel uncomfortable in your current job. Remember: be honest with yourself!

_____

_____

_____

_____

Now that you've identified the root cause of your discomfort, you can start thinking about potential solutions to it—which, obviously, will lie outside your current employment. Remember: a job that makes you uncomfortable is not sustainable in the long run.

### Situation 2: 'I want to quit my job because I'm too comfortable in it.'

Just as people have all kinds of reasons why they actively hate their job, there are dozens of motivations for why someone would want to leave a job that's comfortable but unfulfilling. Picture your current job as a piece in a puzzle that is the workplace culture: if the surrounding pieces don't fit together well, the picture won't look right.

Consider the statements below:

- 'I don't like my boss.'

- 'I don't believe in the message that I am sharing.'

- 'I'm bored and don't feel challenged.'

- 'I don't like the company's culture.'

- 'I don't feel that I'm contributing to a greater cause, the world or the environment.'

As you can see, any one of those reasons could apply to people who hate their jobs. But they are equally applicable to people who simply feel that they've grown 'too comfortable' in their current position. Wanting to quit a comfortable job implies that there's something in that comfortable job that feels uncomfortable—which means that it's simply the flip side of the same coin.

In the space below, write down your own reasons for wanting to leave your too-comfortable job.

_____

_____

_____

_____

Now remember, as I said at the beginning of this section, the career-change journey you're contemplating may not involve leaving your current job at all. So by asking you to consider the two situations above, I'm not telling you that you *have* to quit in order to find your purpose. Not at all!

But what I *do* want you to do is think deeply about your current situation, and to realise that there are all kinds of new, different horizons out there. And, by directly confronting the idea of leaving our current job, we can see that this prospect we often think of as terrifying can actually be exhilarating and liberating, and can point us towards the untapped potential we have inside.

## The three misconceptions about career change

As we've noted above, embarking on a career change is a process that is often associated with fear, not least because so many myths have grown up around it. Let's explore three of the most common misconceptions about career change, and how you can navigate through them.

### Misconception 1: 'Career change is too painful.'

Many people believe that switching careers is a painful process filled with stress and uncertainty. However, this definitely does not have to be the case. With the right attitude and mindset, career change can be an exciting journey that leads to personal and professional growth. Think of it like climbing a mountain: at the base, it looks daunting and insurmountable, filled with potential pitfalls and steep climbs. But as you begin your ascent, you find that the path, while challenging, offers stunning views and a sense of accomplishment with every step.

Take as an example one of my clients, Sarah. Sarah was a marketing manager who felt unfulfilled in her job. She decided to switch to a career in graphic design, something she was passionate about but had no formal training in. By taking online courses and seeking mentorship from a friend in the industry, Sarah not only developed the necessary skills, but also discovered a new sense of purpose and excitement in her work.

**Misconception 2: 'I can't afford to change my career.'**
Another common misconception is that career change is an expensive process that requires a large investment of time and money. However, with careful planning and the right strategy, career change can be affordable and manageable.

You can start by researching affordable online courses or certification programs, or by seeking out mentorship opportunities. Create a budget and prioritise your expenses to ensure that you have the financial stability to support your transition. Many companies also offer professional development programs or tuition reimbursement, which can further alleviate the financial burden.

Another of my clients, John, wanted to transition from his role as an accountant to a software developer. Concerned about the cost of education, he found free coding resources online and joined local coding boot camps that offered scholarships. By networking and finding a mentor, he was able to make the switch without incurring significant costs.

## Misconception 3: 'I don't have the skills to make a career change.'

Many people believe that they don't have the necessary skills or qualifications to switch careers. But, just as with anything, those requirements can be acquired—and often with less work than you think!

For one thing, you need to recognise that many of the skills you already have can be transferred to your new career. Skills like communication, problem-solving and project management are valuable in many fields.

Secondly, learn how to embrace the belief that abilities can be developed through dedication and hard work. A *growth mindset* (which we will cover in greater detail later in this book) will help you overcome obstacles and continue learning.

My client Lisa was a teacher who wanted to become a project manager. Although she initially doubted her abilities, she realised that her organisational skills, ability to manage multiple tasks, and experience in leading a classroom were highly transferable. She took a project management course, earned a certification, and eventually landed a role in her new field.

So, we've just gone over three of the most common misperceptions about career change, and shown how each of them can be overcome. Now, I want you to reflect for a moment and, in the space below, write down:

- Why *you* think career change is painful, or

- Why *you* believe that you can't afford to make a career change, or

- Why *you* feel you don't have the skills necessary to make a career change.

'Wait a minute!' you might be saying right now, 'You just said that all of those are false statements! Why are you asking me to write down things that are wrong??!'

Well, that's just the point: just because we *know* things are wrong doesn't mean we don't *feel* like they're real. So what I want you to do here is reflect on all those things that are holding you back from the career change you want to make. Let out all your limiting beliefs for a few minutes, and then take a break to do something you love before coming back to the book.

Trust me—putting all our fears down in black and white is a great way to start getting them out of our heads!

## Envisioning your career change

### i. Clarifying your vision

Now that you've faced down some of the biggest fears about changing careers, it's time to start defining your *career vision* itself. It can be all too easy to get lost in the day-to-day hustle and lose sight of our long-term goals, which is why it's so important to take a step back and gain clarity on your aspirations. When you have a career vision, you're able to set specific goals and create a plan of action to achieve them.

So, without further ado, write down what you think your career vision is in the space below. (If you think that your vision isn't clear or focused enough, I invite you to take the free Purposeek online course 'Clarify Your Vision'. You can access it at: purposeekcoaching.com.au/career-change-coach ing-online-courses/#vision-focused)

---

---

---

---

## ii. Integrating your life and career vision

Having a career vision is essential to your journey, but that vision can't exist in isolation—it must be connected to your larger *life vision*. After all, your career is only one aspect of your life, and it should help support your broader life goals and aspirations.

Your life vision provides the foundation for your career vision. When you have a clear life vision, it helps you make more-informed decisions about your career, such as choosing a job that aligns with your values and priorities. Without a life vision, you may find yourself in a job that pays well, but doesn't provide a sense of purpose or fulfilment.

Your career vision and life vision should inspire and complement each other. When your career and personal life align with your passions, values and goals, it creates a sense of harmony and balance that leads to overall well-being and success. For example, if your life vision includes travelling the world and experiencing different cultures, your career vision could include working in a field that allows you to travel and work remotely.

In order to find alignment between your life and career visions, start by answering these key questions below. Remember that the more specific and detailed you can be in your answers, the clearer your integrated vision will become. It's also important to revisit and refine your answers on a regular basis as you gain new experiences and insights.

- What do I want to achieve in my personal life?

- How do my personal goals align with the career vision I detailed above?

- What kind of lifestyle do I envision for myself?

- How can my career support my life goals, and vice versa?

### iii. Aligning your career goals and aspirations

Now that you've reflected on your overall life vision, it's time to return to your career vision and start fleshing it out with some specific goals and aspirations. The more detailed you can get with these, the better you will be able to see how you can align your desired career change with your larger life vision.

In the space below, write down your answers to the following questions. Keep in mind that your career goals and aspirations may change over time as you gain new experiences and insights. The key is to stay flexible and open to new opportunities while remaining focused on what truly matters to you.

• What do I want to achieve in my career?




• What kind of impact do I want to make?




• What do I want to learn and experience?

• What skills and strengths do I want to leverage?

---

---

---

• What kind of work environment do I thrive in?

---

---

---

## Finding the five steps for your career change

First off, let me warn you that whenever you see someone telling you that there are only three, or five, or ten steps to be successful in something—unless it's for a cooking recipe—run away, fast! Something as life-altering as a career change can take as many as 100 steps (maybe even more) to accomplish—and some of them will be the wrong ones, some will be super-small, while others will be like giant leaps. As if you could *ever* sum up such a complex process in five steps!

Now, having said that—I want you to write down the five key steps you need to undertake to make your career change a reality.

You may think that I'm joking, but I'm not! While we can't reduce your career-change journey to five simple steps, doing this exercise can encourage you to start thinking about that transformation as something that is more graspable and achievable, not the big scary unknown it was before.

How does it do this? First, it encourages you to articulate your goals in a concrete and actionable way. By breaking down your larger goal into smaller, more manageable steps, you can gain a better understanding of what it will take to achieve your desired outcome. You can also identify potential roadblocks or challenges that may arise, and start thinking about strategies to overcome them.

Second, it allows you to assess your current level of readiness and preparation for a career change. If you are able to identify clear, actionable steps towards your goal right off the bat, it may be an indication that you have been thinking about a career change for a while and have a clear plan in mind. On the other hand, if you struggle to identify specific steps or are unsure of where to start, it may be an indication that you are just beginning your journey or still questioning whether you need or can achieve a career change.

Finally, by acknowledging that what seem like small or, conversely, unrealistic steps can ultimately lead to big changes, this exercise encourages you to think creatively and outside the box when it comes to your career goals. It reminds you that anything is possible with the right mindset, effort and commitment, and that even the smallest steps can lead to big breakthroughs.

So, go for it—write down what you think would be the five key steps you need to undertake for your career change. It doesn't matter if they're small or big, realistic or 'unrealistic'— because what might seem unrealistic today may seem totally achievable tomorrow.

The five steps to accomplish my career change are:

1.

2.

3.

4.

5.

## Conclusion

In this chapter, we explored what career change means to you, de-bunked some of the most common misconceptions about career change, and emphasised the importance of having a clear career vision that aligns with your larger life vision. In the next chapter, we'll focus on the key step of knowing yourself—the foundation of self-empowerment for a successful transition.

# Chapter 3

# Getting to Know You

---

CHANGING CAREERS can be a daunting task, but it can also be an exciting opportunity to start afresh and pursue your passions. However, before making this big leap, it's important to understand who you are and what you want from your career.

Knowing yourself is crucial in determining which career path is the best fit for you. This self-awareness can help you make informed decisions about the type of work you want to do, the company culture you want to be a part of, and the work-life balance you desire.

Getting to know ourself means assessing our present; then our past, and then our future. We start with now because, well, that's where we (always) are! It's the point we've reached in our journey thus far, and the place we're going to embark from as we explore our career-change horizons.

From there, we want to go back in time, to see how our prior experiences, learnings, achievements and setbacks helped shape us into who we are now. Then, we want to combine who we were and who we are, and project ourselves forward to try to imagine ourselves as we will be in our future.

Before we get started, though, I want to ask you to write in the space below your answer to this question:

## Who do you think you are?

This may seem like an impossibly broad or vague question to answer, but I still want you to try to write something down right now; at least two or three sentences. Trust me, it will be important later on!

## Where are you today?

### i. Self-assessment

The first step in figuring out where you are today is doing a self-assessment so that you can see how you view yourself through your own lens. When conducting a self-assessment, there are several key areas to consider:

- **Current skills and strengths**. Evaluate the areas where you excel and where you may need improvement. Understanding your strengths and weaknesses helps you set realistic goals and make informed career decisions.

- **Values and priorities**. Identify what is important to you in your personal and professional life. What are your core beliefs and how do they influence your decisions?

- **Interests and passions**. Reflect on what activities bring you joy and fulfilment, so that you can see how those align with prospective alternative careers.

- **Job satisfaction and work–life balance**. Consider if you are happy with your current job and if it is possible for you to maintain a healthy work–life balance.

Fill out the questionnaire below:

## SELF-ASSESSMENT QUESTIONNAIRE

- Describe yourself in five words.

  _____

  _____

- How do people usually describe you?

  _____

  _____

- What are three things that are really important to you?

  _____

  _____

- What would you say are your five main strengths?

  _____

  _____

- Who are the five people you spend the most time with?

  _____

  _____

- Who are the five people that influence you the most?

  _____

  _____

- Which do you think are the events that have defined you the most, and why?

  _____

  _____

- What are the things about yourself that you are least proud of?

_____

_____

- What were your favourite activities as a child?

_____

_____

- Which one of those activities are you still doing, if any?

_____

_____

- What were your dreams as a child?

_____

_____

- What is your proudest professional moment, and why?

_____

_____

- What are you the most grateful for in your life, and why?

_____

_____

- What do you like about your current job?

_____

_____

- What *don't* you like about your current job?

_____

_____

- If you could, what would you change about your current job?

_____

_____

- How is your current job adding value (e.g. value to your business, your life, the wider community, etc.)?

  _____

  _____

- How is your current job aligned with your values?

  _____

  _____

- How fulfilled are you in your current role?

  _____

  _____

## ii. Solicit feedback from others

Seeking feedback from others is like getting a second opinion from a doctor—it can provide a new perspective and identify potential blind spots. For example, let's say on your self-assessment that you identify one of your main strengths as your communication skills; however, when you ask for feedback from your manager, they mention that you tend to interrupt others in meetings.

But of course, feedback isn't a strictly negative process by any means! Many of us tend to be overly critical of ourselves, or ignorant of some qualities we possess that may be great strengths. Seeking feedback from sources such as a mentor, manager or trusted colleague can reveal those positive parts of ourselves that we minimise or overlook completely.

Working from the email template below, send your feedback request message to at least five friends and/or family members, and three work colleagues. (That's the minimum I'd recommend, but the more the merrier—if you want to cast your net wider, go for it!)

Hi [NAME],

I am currently doing a bit of work on myself, and I could really do with five minutes of your time to give me genuine feedback. Please do not sugar-coat your answers; the more honest you are, the more you would be helping me.

If you could please send me your response by [DATE], that would be very helpful!

1   Please describe me in five words.

2   What are my five superpowers (things I am very good at)?

3   What are three things I could improve on and why?

4   For which type of professional role do you think I'm best suited?

5   What is my reputation (what do other people think of me)?

Thanks again!

Best,

[YOUR NAME]

## How did you get here?

Now that you have a bit more understanding of where you are, it may be interesting to know how you got here in the first place. Reflecting on our past experiences, learnings, achievements and setbacks is an important step towards understanding our present and future selves.

Why is this the case? Firstly, our past experiences can provide clues to our core values and beliefs, which can in turn inform our future decisions and goals.

Secondly, reflecting on our past achievements and setbacks can help us identify our strengths and weaknesses. By acknowledging our successes and failures, we can learn from them and become more confident and resilient in the face of challenges.

Thirdly, reflecting on our past experiences can also help us identify patterns and themes in our lives. For example, if you've always had a passion for sport or art, this may be a clue to your true calling in life. By identifying these patterns, we can gain a better understanding of our passions and purpose, which can inform our career and life decisions.

There are many ways you can go about this process of self-reflection:

- **Journaling** can be a very helpful exercise. Take some time each day to write down your thoughts and feelings about your past experiences, learnings, achievements and setbacks. Write about the situations that had the most impact on you and what you learned from them.

- **Talking to a trusted friend, mentor or therapist** about your past experiences is also something to consider. Having an outside perspective can provide valuable insights and help you gain a new perspective on your life.

- **Meditation or mindfulness exercises** are great methods to help you reflect on your past experiences in a more focused and intentional way. Taking a few minutes each day to sit in silence and reflect on your past experiences can help you gain clarity and insight into your personal growth and development.

For right now, though, I'd like you to complete the exercise below, which asks you to create a timeline of your life, highlighting key moments, achievements and setbacks. Doing this can help you identify patterns and themes in your life and gain a better understanding of your present and future selves.

# YOUR LIFE TIMELINE

- Draw a timeline from your birth to the present day, using the template below.

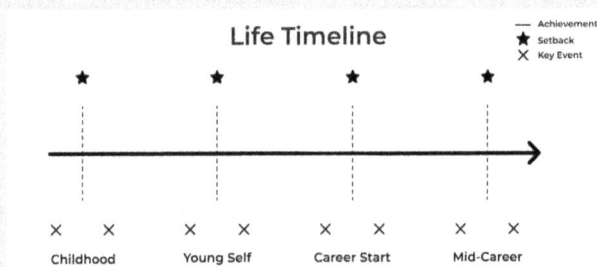

_____

_____

### Life Timeline

— Achievement
★ Setback
✕ Key Event

★        ★        ★        ★

✕    ✕      ✕    ✕      ✕    ✕      ✕    ✕
Childhood      Young Self      Career Start      Mid-Career

- Highlight some of your key moments, achievements and setbacks.

_____

_____

- Reflect on these events and write down what you learned from them in the space below.

_____

_____

- If you can identify any notable patterns or themes in the moments you've highlighted, write them down in the space below.

_____

_____

## Where do you want to go?

Now that you have reflected on your past and present, it's time to focus on your future!

Having a clear vision and direction of where you want to be is essential for achieving success in both your personal and professional life. Without a clear destination in mind, it can be difficult to make informed decisions and take the necessary steps to reach your goals.

One way to gain clarity about your future is to engage in a visualisation exercise. This involves picturing yourself in your ideal future, whether that's five, ten, or however many years from now. Close your eyes and imagine yourself living your best life. What do you see? Where are you? What are you doing? Who are you with? By visualising your ideal future, you can gain clarity about your goals and the steps you need to take to achieve them.

### VISUALISATION EXERCISE: PART I

- Take fifteen minutes to write a brief story in which you are at least ten years older than you are now. Write it as if you were composing a letter to an important person in your life. Describe your life at that moment, explaining why you are happy and why your life has been successful over the last ten or more years.

_____

_____

After completing your letter above, move on to the second part of the exercise below.

## VISUALISATION EXERCISE: PART II

- Looking over your letter, identify any gaps between the happy future you've envisioned and your present situation.

- In the template below, list each of these gaps on a separate line.

- Beneath each gap, write down one immediate action you can take to start closing that gap. You don't have to solve the whole thing in one go—just write down one simple thing you can do now to start moving you towards a resolution.

Gap 1:
Immediate action:

_____

_____

Gap 2:
Immediate action:

_____

_____

By engaging in visualisation exercises such as these, you can gain greater clarity about your goals, values and priorities, and stay motivated and focused on your journey towards success. Remember, your ideal future is within your reach—and, with a clear vision and direction, you can take the necessary steps to achieve it!

## Your Tree of Life

To further explore the concept of visualising, we can use a powerful tool called the Tree of Life, which is a visual metaphor that allows you to reflect on your past, present and future by mapping out the key events, values, skills and relationships that have shaped your life. The goal of this exercise is to reclaim your past and re-envision your future by defining your narrative.

The eight components of the Tree of Life model are as follows:[1]

1  **The Compost Heap**: anything you no longer want to be defined by. These are often sources of trauma, abuse, cultural standards, or anything else that shapes negative thoughts about yourself.

2  **The Roots:** where you come from.

3  **The Ground:** things you choose to do on a weekly basis. These should not be things you are *forced* to do, but rather things you have chosen to do for yourself.

4  **The Trunk:** your skills and values.

5  **The Branches:** your hopes, dreams and wishes.

6  **The Leaves:** the names of those who are important to you in a positive way (friends, family, pets, heroes, etc.).

7  **The Fruits:** the legacies that have been passed on to you. You can start with the names you wrote on leaves and think about what impact they had on you and what they gave you.

8  **The Flowers & Seeds:** the legacies you wish to leave to others.

---

1  Sourced from David Denborough, *Retelling the Stories of Our Lives: Everyday Narrative Therapy to Draw Inspiration and Transform Experience.* Brisbane: W.W. Norton, 2014.

Below, you can see a completed example of a Tree of Life exercise:

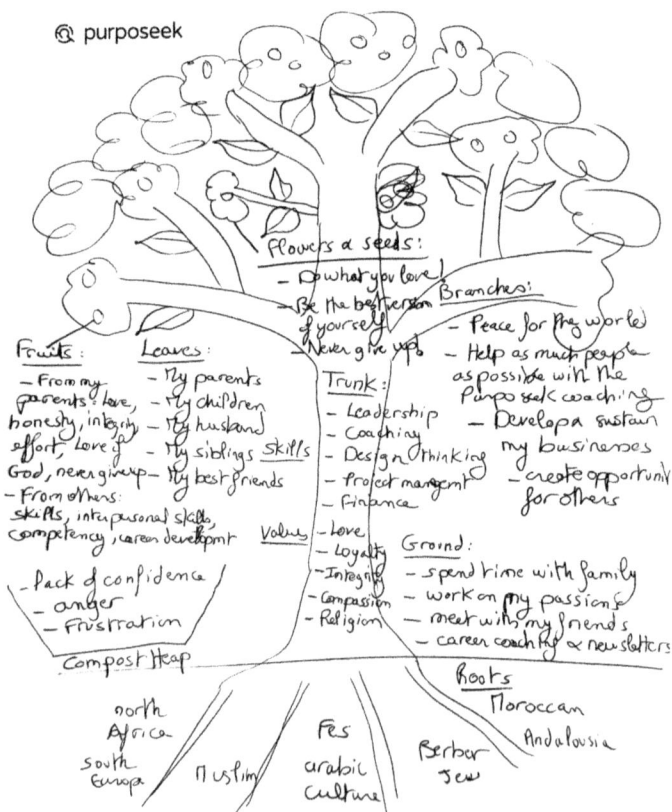

Make sense? Now, let's start drawing your own Tree of Life in the space below.

## YOUR TREE OF LIFE

Once you've completed your Tree of Life, reflect on each element. Which values, skills or activities are most dominant in the narrative you've created? Which of your 'leaves' (important people) are really standing out for you?

Write down all your thoughts and observations in the space below.

## Know your strengths

In the exercises above, we've tried to capture as many aspects of your past, present and envisioned future as possible—the negatives as well as the positives. Now, however, I want you to focus on the latter category by learning how to identify and leverage your strengths.

Your strengths are the unique abilities, talents and qualities that you possess that enable you to excel in certain areas. By leveraging your strengths, you can tap into your full potential, find joy in your work, and make a meaningful impact in the world.

You will already have identified at least some of your key strengths in the self-assessment and feedback exercises. Below, we'll cover some of the other tools you can use to bring those positive attributes to the fore.

One of the most well known talent-assessment tools is the CliftonStrengths method (formerly known as Strengths-Finder) developed by Marcus Buckingham and Donald Clifton, which identifies an individual's top five strengths from a list of thirty-four potential themes, offering a detailed understanding of what they naturally do best.[2]

In the book they developed out of this program, *Now, Discover Your Strengths*, Buckingham and Clifton argue that focusing on your strengths is more effective than trying to improve your weaknesses, as their research indicates that those individuals who are able to harness their inherent strengths are more likely to achieve higher levels of performance and satisfaction in their careers and personal lives, becoming more engaged, productive and happier. The CliftonStrengths method has proved useful in many fields, from corporate training programs to personal development coaching, because it shifts the focus from a deficit-based approach that emphasises fixing weaknesses to a strengths-based approach that encourages individuals to maximise their natural talents.

The Purposeek Coaching Method is also premised on this concept, and has its own unique way to enable you to define your strengths. Below, you'll find a good starter exercise to help you start focusing on the things you truly excel at.

---

2   https://www.gallup.com/cliftonstrengths/en/252137/home.aspx

## DISCOVERING YOUR STRENGTHS

- Take a moment to think about times in your life when you felt most successful and proud. What were you doing in those moments? What skills or talents were you using? Write down at least three instances.

  _____

  _____

- Reach out to three people who know you well (friends, family, colleagues) and ask them to describe what they believe are your top strengths. Encourage them to be specific and provide examples. Write down their responses.

  _____

  _____

- Compare your reflections with the feedback you received. Look for common themes or patterns that emerge. Are there certain skills or qualities that repeatedly come up? List these recurring strengths below.

  _____

  _____

- Answer the following questions to further refine your understanding:

  - Which activities make you feel most energised and engaged?

    _____

    _____

  - What do you find easy to learn and quick to master?

    _____

    _____

- In which areas do you often receive compliments or recognition?

_____

_____

- What tasks or projects do you volunteer for or seek out?

_____

_____

- Based on your reflections, feedback and self-assessment, write a summary of your top five strengths. Describe each strength and provide an example of how you have demonstrated it in the past.

_____

_____

Once you've completed the exercise above, take a short break (or as long as you feel you require!) and then come back and look at your answers. Sit and reflect on them for a while, and then, when you're ready, answer the summary questions below.

What did you learn about yourself from this exercise?

_____

_____

Which discovery surprised you the most, and why?

_____

_____

What are some ways that you can better apply the strengths that you've identified in both your personal and professional lives?

_____

_____

As the philosopher Aristotle once said, 'Knowing yourself is the beginning of all wisdom.' By taking the time to understand your strengths and how to leverage them, you can create a path to success that is both enjoyable and fulfilling.

## So, who do you think you are?

Remember when I asked you this question at the beginning of this chapter? I want you to go back to the answer you wrote down, and read it out loud to yourself.

Now, drawing on the discoveries you've made through completing the exercises and activities in this chapter, I want you to provide an updated answer to that same question:

## Who do you think you are?

In the space below, write a sentence or a brief paragraph that describes who you think you are, approaching that question from any angle you choose; just make sure you include something about both your personal and professional lives. I have a feeling that you will find this new answer is far more detailed and authentic than your initial version.

Write down all your thoughts and observations in the space below.

## Conclusion

Congratulations on completing this chapter! By examining your present self, reflecting on your past experiences, and envisioning your future, you've laid a solid foundation for understanding who you are and what you truly want from your career.

But remember, learning to truly know yourself is not just a one-time activity—it's an ongoing process that will serve as your compass throughout your career-change journey. As you move forward, continue to revisit these exercises, refine your self-assessment, and seek input from those who know you well. This iterative process will keep you grounded and focused on your true self, helping you make more informed and confident decisions.

In the next chapter, we will continue to further refine and focus this process of introspection by introducing a powerful visual tool, which is known as a *mind map*.

# Chapter 4

# Making Your Mind Map— The Four Explorers

IN THE PREVIOUS chapter, you explored different aspects of your identity through self-assessment and feedback. This chapter will take those insights and transform them into a *mind map* that will help you gain a clearer understanding of how these elements interact to support your career aspirations.

A mind map is a visual tool that allows you to organise and connect ideas and information in a creative and non-linear way. It starts with a central idea or topic and branches out into subtopics and related ideas. By creating a mind map, you can easily see the connections between different ideas and how they relate to each other.

For our purposes, we are going to build the mind map for your career-change journey around what I call the 'four explorers':

1 **Values**—the core beliefs and principles that guide your actions and decisions

2 **Passions**—activities or interests that excite you and bring you joy

3  **Desires**—aspirations and goals that drive you towards fulfilment

4  **Needs**—the fundamental elements required for your well-being and happiness

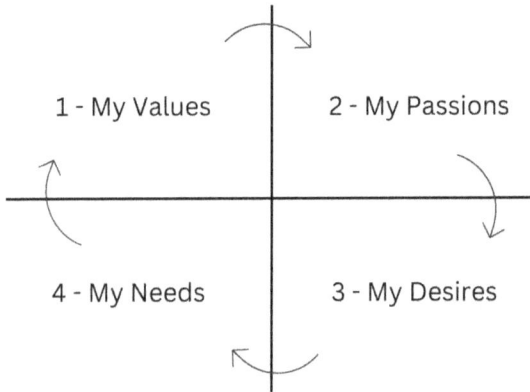

| 1 - My Values | 2 - My Passions |
| 4 - My Needs | 3 - My Desires |

Let's dive deeper into each element and see how they all come together to form a comprehensive map of your inner world, which can lead you towards a truly purpose-driven career.

## Values

Your values are the guiding principles that shape your decisions and actions—the things that you believe in and hold true to, no matter what. Research has shown that aligning your values with your actions can lead to greater happiness and fulfilment not only in your personal life, but in your professional life as well. A study by the *Harvard Business Review* found that individuals who are clear on their values and can live them consistently report greater levels of happiness, lower stress and higher job satisfaction.[3] Public opinion leaders like Brené Brown and Simon Sinek have also emphasised the importance of values in personal and professional growth.

The exercise below is designed to help you define and reflect on your values by presenting a list of value-related words that are grounded in positive psychology. I have sourced the list from the VIA Institute on Character, which is widely recognised for its rigorous work in the field of character strengths.[4] You can also refer to the result from your Tree of Life exercise to include the values you've already identified.

## DEFINE YOUR VALUES

- Identify the **ten values** that are most important to you from the list below.

| | | | | | |
|---|---|---|---|---|---|
| Authenticity | Justice | Determination | Poise | Humanity | Vitality |
| Achievement | Kindness | Excellence | Popularity | Humour | Wealth |
| Adventure | Knowledge | Empathy | Power | Honesty | Wisdom |
| Autonomy | Leadership | Faith | Productivity | Independence | Zest |
| Balance | Learning | Fame | Recognition | Influence | Peace |
| Beauty | Logic | Family | Religion | Inner Peace | Playfulness |
| Boldness | Love | Forgiveness | Reputation | Innovation | Pleasure |
| Challenge | Loyalty | Freedom | Respect | Integrity | |
| Citizenship | Marriage | Friendships | Responsibility | Craftsmanship | |
| Collaboration | Meaningful | Fun | Risk taking | Creativity | |
| Community | Work | Grit | Security | Curiosity | |
| Compassion | Morality | Growth | Self-Respect | Success | |
| Connection | Nature | Happiness | Service | Status | |
| Contribution | Openness | Harmony | Spirituality | Stability | |
| Courage | Optimism | Health | Spontaneity | Trust | |
| | Partnership | | | | |

---

3  Jennifer Tosti-Kharas and Shoshana Dobrow Riza, 'Align Your Values with Your Work'. Harvard Business Review (2019).

4  VIA Institute on Character (n.d.). "The VIA Classification of Character Strengths and Virtues. Retrieved" from https://www.viacharacter.org/

- Narrow down that list of ten values to the **top three values** that are the most important to you at this time.

  _____

  _____

- Incorporate each one of your three selected values into a sentence, so that you can further clarify what each of these values means to you. Make sure to also include an actionable context in which you could bring these values to bear.

**YOUR THREE VALUES**

**Value 1:**
Value:
Sentence:

**Value 2:**
Value:
Sentence:

**Value 3:**
Value:
Sentence:

Now, take some time to reflect on what you wrote about your values, and what these sentences say about you. Reflecting on the sentences you wrote about your values helps you identify patterns and themes in your identity, assess how well your current career aligns with these values, and set intentions for the future. This will enable you to create specific action steps, make more authentic decisions and enhance your self-awareness.

## Passions

Passion is a powerful force that drives us to pursue our dreams and achieve our goals. But what if you haven't found your passion yet? What if you're not sure what truly lights you up and gets you excited? There's a simple solution: start with curiosity.

Curiosity is the spark that ignites our passions. It's the sense of wonder and eagerness to explore that propels us forward and helps us discover new things about ourselves and the world around us. By embracing our curiosity, we open ourselves up to new experiences and possibilities that can lead us to our true passions.

Curiosity begins with exploring. Try new things, visit new places, meet new people. Ask questions and seek out answers. Pay attention to the things that pique your interest and make you feel excited or energised. One famous advocate of this approach is Elizabeth Gilbert, author of *Eat, Pray, Love*. In her later book *Big Magic: Creative Living Beyond Fear*, she encourages readers to embrace their curiosity and see where it takes them, without the pressure of having to find their one true calling.

So if you haven't found your passion yet, don't fret—just explore, experiment, and embrace the unknown. You never know where your curiosity may lead you: it could be the first step towards discovering your true passions and therefore your true career path.

Now, let me ask you this: is there anything, within your personal or professional life, that you feel curious about and that you are willing to explore a bit more? Write down your answer below.

_____

_____

_____

For those who are lucky enough to have a passion, what do you think your passion is? Write down your answer below. (And if 'passion' sounds a bit too intense for you, simply try substituting 'interest' and see what you come up with.)

Take a moment to reflect on how you feel when you think about your passion.

Now, imagine if you could have a career that makes you feel the same way your passion does, whether it's aligned with your passion or something else entirely. Wouldn't that be wonderful, empowering, rejuvenating, exhilarating?

Let's explore how you can translate your passion into a career.

## FINDING A NEW CAREER PATH THROUGH YOUR PASSIONS

- Write down three activities or topics you are deeply passionate about. These should be things you love doing or learning about, even in your free time.

_____

_____

- For each passion, list the skills and talents you use or develop while engaging in them. Consider both hard skills (e.g. writing, coding) and soft skills (e.g. communication, problem-solving).

_____

_____

- Brainstorm different types of careers in which these passions and their accompanying skills are relevant. Write down at least two career options for each passion.

_____

_____

- For each passion, choose one of the career options that you identified. Reflect on how well these align with your values and long-term goals, and consider the typical roles, responsibilities and qualifications needed for each of these careers. (You can do some additional research on this later if needed.)

_____

- Select the career option that is most appealing to you. Outline a basic action plan with steps you need to take to transition into this career (e.g. additional education, networking, gaining relevant experience).

_____

In the table below, you can see an example of a completed version of this exercise.

**Passion**: Cooking
- Skills: creativity, time management, attention to detail
- Careers: chef, food blogger

**Passion**: Writing
- Skills: storytelling, grammar, research
- Careers: author, content writer

**Passion**: Fitness
- Skills: Coaching, motivation, anatomical knowledge
- Careers: personal trainer, fitness instructor

Now, even though you've drafted a basic action plan, don't start actioning anything yet. Keep it on paper for now, and we will come back to it later in the book.

## Desires

Desires are the things that we long for and crave—the things that bring us joy and make us feel alive. They may be small or large, simple or complex, but they are always deeply personal. Essentially, your desires are a roadmap to your true self: when you recognise and honour these desires, you align your actions and choices with your core identity, leading to a more genuine and fulfilling life.

While following your desires may seem like an obvious path towards happiness and fulfilment, there are conflicting opinions on the matter. Some argue that following your desires can lead to selfishness and a lack of consideration for others; others argue that desires can be fleeting and may not lead to long-term satisfaction. The great philosopher Aristotle, for example, believed that true happiness comes from living a life of virtue and moral excellence, rather than solely pursuing our desires. He argued that we should strive for a balance between our desires and our responsibilities to others and society.

On the other hand, contemporary positive psychology research has found that pursuing our desires can lead to greater well-being and life satisfaction. Some studies have shown that when individuals align their goals and actions with their personal desires and values, they experience greater levels of happiness and fulfilment.[5]

So, how can we reconcile these seemingly conflicting perspectives? In my opinion, it's important to recognise that following your desires does not necessarily mean ignoring your responsibilities to others or society. Rather, it means pursuing your desires in a way that is aligned with your values and that does not harm others.

It's also important to note that desires don't have to be solely focused on personal fulfilment. Many people feel a deep desire to make a positive impact in the world and contribute to something greater than themselves. This desire for meaning and purpose can be just as powerful and important

---

5   e.g., Oishi, S., Diener, E., Suh, E., & Lucas, R. E. (1999). 'Value as a moderator in subjective well-being'. *Journal of Personality*, 67(1), 157-184.

as any more self-centred desire. For example, if your desire is to start your own business, you can do so in a way that benefits your community and provides value to others. Or, if your desire is to travel the world, you can do so in a way that respects local cultures and promotes sustainable tourism.

For me, desire isn't about chasing fleeting, superficial whims that come and go. Instead, it represents a profound and genuine connection with our true selves. A deep sense of desire is intrinsically linked to our purpose and inner motivation. The reason we aim to follow our desires is because they are what naturally surface and are easily identifiable. However, the goal is not to pursue these desires blindly; rather, we should use them as starting points to uncover the deeper motivations behind them, which can often lead us to our true purpose.

The exercise below is designed to help you reflect on your desires and what truly makes you happy. And, to indicate the spirit in which we should be speaking of our desires, I've titled the exercise with an inverse of that self-punishing old motto 'no pain, no gain.'

## NO JOY, NO GAIN!

- Think about what brings you joy. If you're struggling to find answers right off the bat, don't worry. For many of us, we're so deeply immersed in our daily routines that the concept of 'joy' often hardly comes to our minds!

**Here's a tip:** think about the twelve-year-old you, and what brought you joy then. Obviously, your joys will have changed or evolved considerably since then, but tapping back into that simpler, more elemental form of desire can help lead you towards the things that truly bring you joy in the present.

When you've taken the time you need to think about this question deeply and seriously, write down what you've discovered in the space below.

_____

_____

* Now that you've identified some of the things that bring you joy, the next step is to incorporate those activities into your daily or weekly routine. Start small with one or two activities, then gradually increase as you become more comfortable. Periodically reflect on how these activities impact your mood, and adjust your schedule as needed to ensure it remains fulfilling and practical.

Here's an example of such a schedule to help get you thinking:

## WEEKLY 'JOY SCHEDULE'

| Day | Morning Activity (7am–7:30am) | Evening Activity |
| --- | --- | --- |
| Monday | Meditation, prayer or yoga | 6pm–7pm: Cooking favourite meal |
| Tuesday | Journaling | 6pm–7pm: Reading a book |
| Wednesday | Walk in the park | 6pm–7pm: Hobby (e.g. painting, knitting...) |
| Thursday | Gratitude practice | 7pm–8pm: Catching up with a friend |
| Friday | Listening to a podcast | 6pm–7pm: Movie night or TV show |
| Saturday | 9am–10am: Exercise (e.g. gym, run, cycling...) | 2pm–3pm: Gardening or outdoor activity |
| Sunday | 9am–10am: Creativity activity (e.g. drawing, writing...) | 3pm–4pm: Family time or community activity |

- Now, do a preliminary sketch of your own weekly 'joy schedule' below.

| Day | Morning Activity (7am–7:30am) | Evening Activity |
|---|---|---|
| Monday | | |
| Tuesday | | |
| Wednesday | | |
| Thursday | | |
| Friday | | |
| Saturday | | |
| Sunday | | |

Understanding and incorporating your desires into your daily routine is not just about enhancing personal happiness—it's also a crucial step in your career-change journey. By recognising what truly brings you joy and integrating these activities into your life, you gain deeper insight into what you value most. This clarity will guide you in making informed career decisions that align with your true passions and desires.

## Needs

While our desires, as we've discussed above, are far from fleeting or surface-level, needs are those things that are absolutely fundamental to our survival and happiness. Vital needs, such as breathing and eating, are non-negotiable for our survival. Essential needs, like a safe environment, a home and a supportive family, are crucial for our happiness and fulfilment.

In this section, we are going to focus on the six universal needs, as they form the bedrock of a fulfilled and purposeful life. Understanding and addressing these needs ensures that we build a life that is stable, satisfying and aligned with our core values.

1  **Certainty**: assurance you can avoid pain and gain pleasure (e.g. income, job security)

2  **Uncertainty/variety**: the need for the unknown, change, new stimuli (e.g. holidays, going out, meeting new people)

3  **Significance**: feeling unique, important, special, needed (e.g. recognition from others or yourself)

4  **Connection/love**: a strong feeling of closeness or union with someone or something

5  **Growth**: an expansion of capacity, capability or understanding (e.g. new learnings)

6  **Contribution**: a sense of service and focus on helping, giving to and supporting others

Take a moment to think about each of these needs and how they apply to your life. What are some examples of how you've experienced each of these needs in the past? How important are they to you?

Now, on a scale of 1 to 5 (with 5 being the highest), rate how well each of these needs is currently being met in your life. Be honest with yourself—there are no right or wrong answers here.

Universal needs scoring

Once you've scored each need, take a look at your results. Which needs are being met at a high level, and which are not? These are your primary needs—the ones that are most important to you and that you should prioritise.

By taking the time to assess and prioritise your needs, you're gaining a deeper understanding of what truly matters to you. Desires often change depending on your context, environment and personal growth. However, your needs are more stable and don't fluctuate as much, as they are fundamental to your well-being and rooted in your core values and basic human requirements.

The difference between desires and needs is that while desires might bring short-term pleasure, meeting your needs is likely to provide long-term satisfaction and fulfilment. In the context of a career change, aligning your new path with your core needs ensures a more profound and lasting sense of purpose and happiness. By understanding and prioritising your needs, you are setting the stage for a career that not only excites you, but also sustains your well-being over time.

## Reading your mind map

Now that you've identified and gained a deeper understanding of your values, passions, desires and needs, it's time to go back to your mind map and complete each quadrant with your findings. Take some time to reflect on how each aspect of your life connects with and influences the others. Consider how your values and passions can inform your desires and needs, and vice versa.

As you complete each quadrant, be open to making adjustments and refinements based on your newfound insights. Remember, this is a process of self-discovery and growth, and it's okay if your thoughts and feelings evolve over time.

By integrating your newfound knowledge into your mind map, you'll have a powerful tool that reflects your true self and can guide you towards discovering your purpose. So take your time, be thorough, and, most importantly, be true to yourself.

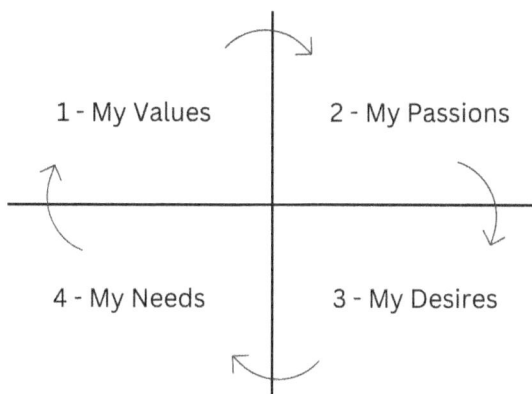

|                  |                   |
| ---------------- | ----------------- |
| 1 - My Values    | 2 - My Passions   |
| 4 - My Needs     | 3 - My Desires    |

## Conclusion

Completing your mind map not only helps you visualise the intercon-nectedness of your values, passions, desires and needs, but also provides a comprehensive overview of who you are at your core. This clarity is essential for making informed decisions that align with your true self. In the next chapter, we're going to assess each of these aspects through three different lenses:

- Your *environment*, to understand how external factors influence you;
- Your *talents*, those abilities that you have a natural inclination for; and
- The *meaning* those four explorers have for you, so that we can grasp the drivers behind your goals and aspirations.

# Chapter 5

# Making Your Mind Map—
# Discovering Your Drivers

NOW THAT YOU'VE completed your mind map, let's introduce a critical new element that will complete this powerful tool. In the previous chapter, we covered the 'four explorers'—your values, passions, desires and needs—which helped illuminate key dimensions of who you are. But to truly uncover your intrinsic motivation and understand what drives you, we need to shift our focus to the centre of your mind map. Here, we will place three essential concepts: *environment*, *talent* and *meaning*.

This chapter will be all about exploring these three concepts and linking them to your intrinsic motivation. Below, you'll see the complete version of the mind map, with *environment*, *talent* and *meaning* now positioned at its centre. These concepts will guide your journey towards a purpose-driven career, helping you make decisions that align with both who you are and where you want to go.

Intrinsic motivation refers to the inner drive or desire to engage in an activity for its own sake, rather than for any external rewards or incentives. It is driven by a sense of enjoyment, satisfaction and personal fulfilment, rather than for external rewards such as money or status.

```
              1 - My Values                    2 - My Passions

                            Environment

                              Talent

                              Meaning

              4 - My Needs                     3 - My Desires
```

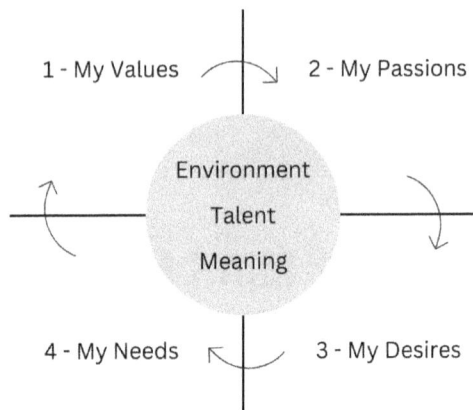

One of the leading researchers on intrinsic motivation is Dan Pink, who has written extensively on the topic in his book *Drive: The Surprising Truth About What Motivates Us.*[6] Pink argues that traditional, top-down methods of motivation, such as external rewards or punishments, can actually undermine intrinsic motivation and lead to reduced creativity, productivity and overall job satisfaction.

According to Pink, intrinsic motivation is driven by three key factors: autonomy, mastery and purpose.

*Autonomy* denotes our ability to make decisions and control our work. *Mastery* refers to the desire to improve and develop one's skills and abilities. *Purpose* is a sense of connection to a larger goal or mission, and the belief that one's work has a meaningful impact on the world.

Pink's work highlights the importance of creating work environments that foster intrinsic motivation by giving employees more autonomy, opportunities for skill development and growth, and a sense of purpose in their work.

---

6    Dan Pink, *Drive: The Surprising Truth About What Motivates Us.* New York: Riverhead Books, 2009.

By focusing on these factors, organisations can not only increase employee engagement and satisfaction, but also drive greater productivity and success.

Intrinsic motivation is not just important in the workplace, however. It is a fundamental aspect of human nature, and is tied to our sense of self-worth and personal fulfilment. By engaging in activities that we find intrinsically rewarding, such as pursuing hobbies or learning new skills, we can enhance our overall well-being and sense of purpose in life.

So, how do you go about finding your intrinsic motivation?

## Finding your intrinsic motivation

Following the lead of Dan Pink, we're going to use the three factors of autonomy, mastery and purpose as guides to help you identify your intrinsic motivation. By examining and analysing how each of these factors functions across three different fields of activity in your life, we will work to pinpoint where you need to concentrate your efforts.

First, I want you to select three activities that you enjoy doing:

1   One related to your personal life that benefits you;
2   One related to your personal life that benefits others; and,
3   One related to your work.

Then, for each of these activities, I want you to reflect on the sense of autonomy, mastery and purpose that you have when practising them. Let me give you an example so you have a better idea of the questions I want you to ask yourself.

Say that the activity you select related to your personal life is cooking. Here are some potential questions you could ask yourself to determine your relative levels of autonomy, mastery and purpose in this activity:

### Autonomy

- How much control do you have over the cooking process? Are you able to choose what you want to cook, how you want to cook it and when you want to cook it?

- Do you feel like you have the freedom to experiment with new ingredients or techniques when you cook?

### Mastery

- How skilled do you feel when it comes to cooking? Do you think you have a good understanding of the basic techniques and ingredients?

- Are you always striving to improve your cooking skills? If so, how do you go about doing that?

- What are some examples of dishes that you've mastered and feel confident making?

### Purpose

- What drives you to cook? Is it the joy of feeding others and seeing them enjoy your food?

- Do you have any specific goals related to cooking? For example, do you want to open your own restaurant one day?

- How does cooking align with your values and personal beliefs?

Your turn now! Use the space below to record your thoughts on the levels of autonomy, mastery and purpose you have in each of your selected activities.

## IDENTIFY YOUR DRIVERS—STEP 1

i) Personal activity:
- Autonomy:
- Mastery:
- Purpose:

ii) Activity for others:
- Autonomy:
- Mastery:
- Purpose:

iii) Work-related activity:
- Autonomy:
- Mastery:
- Purpose:

Now, take a few minutes to review your responses. For each activity, which of the three factors of autonomy, mastery and purpose is most pronounced, and which one is most lacking?

## IDENTIFY YOUR DRIVERS—STEP 2

Write down the strongest and weakest factors for each activity:

i) Personal activity:
- Strongest factor:
- Weakest factor:

ii) Activity for others:
- Strongest factor:
- Weakest factor:

iii) Work-related activity:
- Strongest factor:
- Weakest factor:

Now that you've identified which factor is lacking for each activity, it's time to consider how you can take action to strengthen that factor.

Let's go back to the cooking example we used above. After completing Step 2 of the exercise, let's say that you've realised that the factor of *mastery* is missing. What are some ways you could go about enhancing this aspect of the activity? You could:

- Take a cooking course to learn new techniques and improve your skills

- Experiment with different recipes and ingredients to challenge yourself and expand your knowledge

- Seek feedback from others, such as friends or family, to get an outside perspective on your cooking and identify areas for improvement

There are all kinds of other potential remedies as well, but hopefully that gives you a few ideas! Now, let's apply this approach to the three activities you selected in Step 1.

## IDENTIFY YOUR DRIVERS—STEP 3

For each selected activity, write down potential ways you could enhance the factor that is most lacking:

i) Personal activity:
- Weakest factor:
- Potential remedies:

ii) Activity for others:
- Weakest factor:
- Potential remedies:

iii) Work-related activity:
- Weakest factor:
- Potential remedies:

Well done! Now that we've examined the relative strength of those three factors within each activity individually, it's time to examine the common denominators in each of those factors across your three activities.

For example, let's say you selected the following three activities in Step 1 of the exercise:

**Personal activity**: playing guitar

**Activity for others**: volunteering at a local animal shelter

**Work-related activity**: managing a marketing project

Now, let's examine the shared themes that crop up when we examine each of the three factors across each activity.

For **autonomy**, the common denominator could be the *ability to have creative control*.

- When you're playing guitar, you have the autonomy to choose the songs you want to play and how you want to play them.

- When volunteering at the local animal shelter, you have the autonomy to choose the shelter where you want to contribute and the specific tasks you want to undertake.

- For the marketing project, perhaps the thing you value most is your ability to choose the messaging and design.

For **mastery**, the common denominator could be the *desire to improve your skills and knowledge*.

- In playing guitar, you can work to develop your finger-picking or chord transitions.

- At the shelter, you can learn how to administer medication and advance your animal-handling skills.

- On the marketing project, perhaps you can use it as an opportunity to enhance your expertise in such aspects as copywriting or design.

For **purpose**, the common denominator could be your *desire to make a positive impact*.

- Your guitar-playing could be a means to share your music with others and bring them some joy.

- With your shelter work, obviously, you are helping animals in need and contributing to their well-being.

- With the marketing project, perhaps you're fortunate enough to be promoting a product or service that can improve people's lives.

Got the idea? Now it's time for you to tackle this question for the three activities you selected.

## IDENTIFY YOUR DRIVERS—STEP 4

In the cells of the grid below, write down specific instances where you've experienced autonomy, mastery and purpose within each type of activity. Then, use the last column to identify the common denominators across your three activities for each factor.

| Factor | Personal Activity | Activity for Others | Work-Related Activity | Common Denominators |
|---|---|---|---|---|
| Autonomy | | | | |
| Mastery | | | | |
| Purpose | | | | |

Before we move to the next step, we need to connect the concepts of autonomy, mastery and purpose with the broader themes I introduced at the beginning of the chapter:

*environment, talent* and *meaning.* Understanding how these concepts naturally flow into one another will help you translate your insights into actionable steps.

## From autonomy to environment

When autonomy is a key factor in your activities, it indicates a need for an environment where you have control over your actions, decisions and creative processes. If autonomy was a common denominator, your ideal environment might be one that offers flexibility, freedom to innovate, and opportunities to work independently. This could be found in a start-up, freelance work, or a role that allows for self-management.

## From mastery to talent

Mastery involves the desire to continually improve and develop your skills. If mastery consistently shows up in your activities, it suggests that you thrive when focusing on your strengths and refining areas where you naturally excel. This connection highlights your talent—what you are good at and passionate about improving. For example, if you seek to enhance your knowledge in a specific field, it indicates both a talent and a drive for growth in that area.

## From purpose to meaning

Purpose revolves around doing something that has significance and impact. When purpose is central to your activities, it suggests that you are motivated by work that aligns with your values and contributes to something larger than yourself. Meaning emerges from engaging in activities that resonate with your inner values and bring fulfilment. If your purpose is to make a positive impact, the meaning you find in your work will likely be tied to roles that allow you to contribute to societal good or help others.

Now it's your turn! In the exercise below, I want you to reflect on your common denominators in terms of autonomy, mastery and purpose, and translate these insights into identifying your ideal environment, your natural talent, and what is meaningful to you.

## IDENTIFY YOUR DRIVERS—STEP 5

Write down your ideal environment, what you are good at or have a talent for, and what is really meaningful to you.

Your 3 drivers in terms of:

1  Your ideal environment
2  Your talent
3  What is meaningful to you

When you've finished the exercise above, go back to your mind map and add those drivers you've identified in relation to your environment, talent and meaning to the space provided. This is the vital centre around which your values, passions, needs and desires orbit.

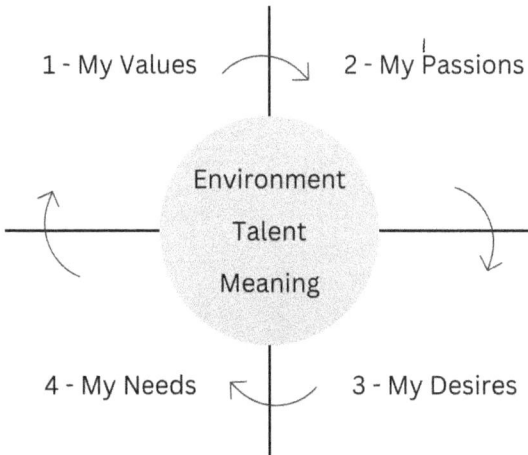

1 - My Values        2 - My Passions

Environment
Talent
Meaning

4 - My Needs        3 - My Desires

## Conclusion

In the previous chapter, we charted the four dimensions of your mind map by defining your four explorers—your values, passions, desires and needs. In this chapter, we applied the concept of intrinsic motivation to complete that map by defining your drivers, which we've categorised into three essential areas: environment, talent and meaning.

With this powerful visual representation of your inner self as a foundation, you're now ready to take the next step in your journey. In the upcoming chapter, we'll explore the concept of 'flow', where you'll learn to harness the energy and focus that come from being fully engaged in what you love. With your drivers clearly defined, you're now ready to discover how to channel them into experiences that bring you into a state where your talents and passions effortlessly align.

# Chapter 6

# Finding Your Flow

NOW THAT YOUR mind map is complete and you have a clear understanding of your intrinsic motivation, it's time to dive into another concept that builds on everything you've uncovered so far: *flow*. This is my favourite topic in this whole book, and you'll soon see why.

'Flow' is a term coined by psychologist Mihaly Csikszentmihalyi to describe a state of complete immersion in an activity, in which we lose track of time and become completely absorbed in what we are doing. It's a state where we feel a deep sense of satisfaction and fulfilment, and often occurs when we are using our skills to their fullest potential.

Csikszentmihalyi's research has shown that people who experience flow on a regular basis are more likely to be creative, productive and happy, and that those who experienced flow on a regular basis are also more likely to report a high level of life satisfaction.[7] This is because when you are in a state of flow, you are doing something that you love, and you are doing it well.

---

7   Mikhail Csikszentmihalyi, *Flow: The Psychology of Optimal Experience*. New York: Harper & Row, 1990.

One of the many benefits of being in a state of flow is that it can help you reduce the number of hours you work. When you are fully engaged in a task, you are able to work more efficiently and effectively. This means that you can accomplish more in less time, leaving you with more time to pursue other interests or simply relax and enjoy life.

Public opinion leaders such as Tony Robbins and Tim Ferriss have spoken about the benefits of being in flow. Robbins has said that being in a state of flow is one of the keys to success, and that it is important to find activities that allow you to experience it on a regular basis. Ferriss, for his part, has developed strategies for creating a state of flow.

So, how do you go about achieving this?

The first step is to identify activities that you *enjoy and are passionate about*. These could be hobbies, sports, creative pursuits or work-related tasks. Whatever they are, though, it is crucial that they align with your interests and values, to ensure that you stay motivated and engaged.

Another important factor to consider is the level of *control* you have over the activity. Flow is more likely to occur during an activity when you can make decisions that positively impact the outcome. Therefore, choosing activities that allow for creativity and decision-making can increase the likelihood of experiencing flow.

In addition, it is important to choose activities that *require your full attention*. This means avoiding activities that are prone to (or even defined by) distractions, such as checking emails or social media, and selecting those that will allow you to fully immerse yourself in the task at hand. Examples are numerous, and range from artistic pursuits (playing a musical instrument, writing, painting) to physical activities (running, swimming, rock climbing) to tasks requiring scientific or technological expertise (programming, coding).

So, let's get started! In the space below, list three activities that you enjoy and are passionate about. These could be related to your personal life, work or hobbies.

_____

_____

_____

Now that you've identified some activities, you need to assess whether they have the potential to provide a flow experience. According to Csikszentmihalyi, flow occurs when there is a balance between the challenge of the activity and your skill level. Therefore, it is important to choose activities that are neither too easy nor too difficult for you, but just challenging enough to keep you engaged and focused.

## ASSESSING YOUR FLOW ACTIVITIES

- Break down each activity you identified in the previous exercise into smaller tasks.

_____

_____

- Assess the level of challenge each task presents.

_____

_____

- Identify adjustments you can make to ensure a balance that maximises your potential for flow.

_____

_____

After completing the exercise above, you should have one or more activities that have the potential to put you into a flow state. Now what you need to do is make room in your schedule to practise this activity at least once a week. This isn't just about adding more tasks to your already busy calendar— it's about carving out dedicated time for those activities that truly engage and energise you.

Start by following the steps below:

## SCHEDULING YOUR FLOW ACTIVITIES

- Look back at the activities you've identified, and choose one or more to focus on.

- Take a look at your current weekly schedule. Identify some times that you could realistically dedicate to practising your chosen flow activity.

- Select at least one time slot each week when you can practise your flow activity. Treat this as a non-negotiable appointment—just as important as any work meeting or personal commitment.

- Write down your chosen time slots in your calendar or planner. Make a commitment to yourself to stick to these times and fully engage in your flow activity.

- After a few weeks of practising your flow activity, reflect on how it feels. Are you consistently reaching a state of flow? If not, consider adjusting your activity or schedule to better support the flow experience.

## Conclusion

Once you experience that sweet flow state, you'll be hooked! As you immerse yourself in flow, your working hours can magically reduce because the focus and efficiency gained from being in flow can amplify your productivity even as your overall well-being is enhanced. Flow is a powerful tool that will keep you motivated and focused as you move forward on your career-change journey.

Now that you've learned how to harness the power of flow, it's time to turn our attention outward. In the next chapter, we'll explore how your environment, relationships and external influences play a crucial role in shaping your career and life decisions. Understanding these factors will help you build a supportive ecosystem that aligns with your purpose and keeps you on the path to success.

# Chapter 7

# Navigating External Factors

EVEN AS YOU find your flow and prepare to unleash your newfound superpowers upon the world, it's important to consider the external factors that shape our lives. We can't always flow as freely as we like, effortlessly skimming over the twists and turns that fate throws our way. The simple fact is that many factors in our lives are beyond our control, and can exert a considerable influence or impact on our desired path to fulfilment.

But don't worry—despite the challenges that lie ahead, there are strategies and approaches you can employ to help you overcome them. It's all about finding your inner strength, adapting to the ever-changing landscape, and standing tall in the face of adversity. Remember, even though we can't control external circumstances, we can control how we respond to them.

When considering career change, the first step in exerting that control is to take stock of some of the major external factors that could impact our success—not, I stress, to scare ourselves out of attempting the shift in the first place, but rather to understand the terrain that we'll be heading into. Three of the most crucial are:

- **Financial needs**. I would highly recommend that you conduct a thorough assessment of your financial situation (ideally with the guidance of a financial professional) before making any drastic alterations to your lifestyle. Take into account your current living expenses (such as housing, food, bills, family commitments and education) as well as your current savings and potential future savings.

- **Personal commitments**. It's important to recognise the impact that any life or career change may have on your various responsibilities and obligations to others, and how you can effectively manage them while striving towards your goals. These commitments can range from caring for family members to maintaining relationships, pursuing personal hobbies, engaging in community activities, and more.

- **The current business environment**. Understanding your environment can help you make informed decisions and adapt your plans accordingly to optimise your chances of success. Consider such factors as the job market, industry trends, your geographical location, the support networks available to you, and so on.

All of the above are important steps to take as you embark on your career-change journey. But, as I said way back in the earliest chapters, this book is not intended as a step-by-step manual, but rather as a resource and a spark of inspiration for you to design that journey for yourself.

That's why, in this chapter, we will focus more on managing personal and workplace relationships—key external influences that can significantly impact your career-change journey. These are the external factors we encounter daily, and how we handle them can either propel us forward or hold us back.

## Dealing with toxic people in your work environment

As the great author and motivational speaker Jim Rohn once said, 'You are the average of the five people you spend the most time with.' By that logic, surrounding yourself with positive individuals—those whom you admire, look up to, and aspire to be more like—is crucial for your growth and happiness.

Positive people uplift and inspire you. They provide support, motivation and constructive feedback, creating an environment where you can thrive. On the other side, toxic people— individuals who consistently exhibit negative behaviours, such as being overly critical, manipulative or unsupportive— can drain your energy, lower your self-esteem and hinder your progress.

What are some of the identifying traits of positive and toxic people?

| Positive people | Toxic people |
| --- | --- |
| **Are supportive and encouraging.** They celebrate your successes and offer support during tough times. | **Are negative and critical.** They often focus on the negative and criticise you without offering solutions. |
| **Give constructive feedback.** They provide honest criticism aimed at helping you grow and improve. | **Drain energy.** You feel exhausted or anxious after interacting with them. |
| **Have a positive attitude.** They maintain a positive outlook and inspire you to do the same. | **Are jealous.** They may be envious of your successes and try to undermine your achievements. |
| **Are inspiring.** They motivate you to achieve your goals and aspire to be better. | **Are unsupportive.** They are rarely there for you when you need support or encouragement. |

To fully understand how our environment influences our career-change journey, it's essential to recognise both the positive and negative forces at play. While surrounding ourselves with positive people is crucial for our growth and well-being, it's equally important to address the challenges posed by toxic individuals. These negative influences can have a significant impact on our progress, often more so than we realise. This is why it's necessary to develop strategies for dealing with them effectively. By doing so, we can protect our mental and emotional well-being, stay focused on our goals, and maintain the positive momentum we've worked so hard to build.

While it may not be possible to completely avoid toxic people, you can strategically create boundaries and seek out opportunities to create a safe distance between yourself and their negative influence. By establishing boundaries, you empower yourself to filter out the noise and focus on the insights that truly resonate with your unique journey. As Brené Brown says, 'Daring to set boundaries is about having the courage to love ourselves even when we risk disappointing others.'

What are some of the boundaries we can establish between ourselves and toxic people that can keep us protected without potentially aggravating the toxicity?

- **Time boundaries**. If it's necessary for you to meet with a toxic person, determine in advance how long you're willing to spend with them, and create an exit strategy. Having a predetermined time limit will help you maintain control over your own schedule and ensure that the encounter doesn't drag on longer than necessary.

- **Space boundaries.** Determine the degree of physical or emotional space you feel you need to maintain between yourself and the individual in question, and devise strategies to achieve that distance. One approach could be to consciously avoid situations where you might cross paths. Or you could make sure you have a 'buffer buddy' who can provide an excuse to exit the interaction if needed.

- **Feedback boundaries.** While we've previously established how important it is to listen to and consider the feedback of others, remember that you don't have to accept advice from just anyone who offers it! It's vital to discern whose opinions truly align with your values and goals.

A helpful tip to manage unwanted feedback is to politely acknowledge it without committing to action. You can say something like, 'Thank you for your input, I'll consider it,' and then decide later whether it truly resonates with your own direction. This allows you to maintain control over the feedback you act on without feeling pressured to please everyone.

Remember, setting boundaries is an act of self-care and self-respect. By proactively defining your limits, you empower yourself to prioritise your well-being and maintain healthy relationships.

## Creating your own positive environment

While the strategies we've discussed above are ways to manage toxic people in our environment, our end goal is to actively create a positive environment for ourselves instead of just mitigating the harm that can be done by negativity. You deserve to be in an environment that promotes positivity and allows you to thrive, and the key to this lies in recognising your own worth and surrounding yourself with people who uplift and inspire you. Ultimately, *you* are the one who has the power to take control of your own happiness and create a fulfilling work life.

Let's start by identifying what that fulfilling work life would look like in your ideal world. Taking the time to envision your ideal work life is more than just a creative exercise—it's a powerful step towards clarity in your career-change journey. By visualising what truly makes you happy and fulfilled in a work environment, you can better understand the types of roles, companies and industries that align with your values and aspirations. This process not only sharpens your focus on what you want but also helps you identify potential obstacles and opportunities as you move forward.

## CREATE YOUR POSITIVE ENVIRONMENT

Describe what your ideal work environment would be like in terms of the following:

Industry

_____

_____

Role

_____

_____

Activities

_____

_____

Leadership

_____

_____

Work relationships

_____

_____

Location

_____

_____

Compare the answers you listed above with your current work situation. Which of the ideal conditions listed does your current job provide you? This comparison will help you identify the areas that need change.

_____

_____

Now list the aspects of your current job that do *not* align with your vision. These are the areas that require attention as you prepare for your career-change journey.

_____

_____

Consider what steps you can take to transition from your current situation to your ideal work environment. These steps might include upskilling, networking, or exploring new opportunities in your desired field.

_____

_____

That final step in the exercise above is perhaps the most important. Remember, in order to start moving closer to your ideal career, it's crucial to start taking actionable steps *today*.

Now, from your reply to that final question, *choose one specific change you can make that will bring you closer to your ideal work environment*. This could be as simple as researching new job opportunities, reaching out to a mentor in your desired field, or beginning a new course to develop a necessary skill.

Finally, *commit to this action by setting a deadline*. Mark it on your calendar and share your goal with someone who can support you, such as a friend, family member or coach. Their encouragement will help keep you accountable and motivated as you take this important step towards your career change.

## Conclusion

As you navigate your career-change journey, it's crucial to recognise that while your internal motivations and passions are essential, external factors also play a significant role in shaping your path. This chapter has highlighted the importance of understanding and managing these external influences—whether they come in the form of financial needs, personal commitments, or the people you interact with daily.

By developing strategies to handle toxic influences and actively working to create a positive environment, you're not just reacting to the world around you, but taking control of your future. You're setting the stage for a career that aligns with your values, talents and desires, ultimately leading to a more fulfilling and purpose-driven life.

And, speaking of purpose, it's time that we move on to one of the most pivotal steps in this book: creating a *purpose statement* that will serve as your North Star on your career-change journey.

# Chapter 8

# Defining Your
# Purpose Statement

AS WE LAUNCH into this chapter, I want us to start by revisiting an exercise you've already completed.

Remember in Chapter 3 when I first asked you to answer the question, 'Who do you think you are?' I'd like you to take a moment to go back to your answer, and read it out loud to yourself.

Then, go back to the end of Chapter 3, where I asked you to answer that question again. Read it out loud to yourself.

Can you predict what I'm going to ask you next? Yep, that's right—I want you to answer, for the third time,

## Who do you think you are?

I know, I know—there are surely a number of you right now who are tempted to groan, roll your eyes, and turn to the next page after being asked to perform the same exercise yet again. Before you do, though, just think about how far you've come since Chapter 3—all the revelations and self-knowledge you've gained through the exercises and activities you completed in all the other chapters that came after you first replied to that question. So, I really encourage you to think deeply and seriously about this question, and answer it one more time.

Now, why did I ask you to do this exercise again? Because, having now gained greater clarity and understanding of your values, passions, interests, desires and needs, returning to this question will enable you to unlock a crucial piece of the puzzle in your career-change journey—your purpose.

What exactly is purpose? This is the crucial question we asked at the very beginning of this book. Think of it as the reason you get out of bed in the morning. It's the driving force behind everything you do and the motor that will get you to the ultimate goal you want to achieve.

What is life like without purpose? Imagine you're playing a game of basketball. You're dribbling down the court, and suddenly you realise that you have no idea where the hoop is. You don't know which direction to go, so you end up just aimlessly dribbling around the court. You wouldn't have any chance of scoring a point, and would probably end up feeling defeated and discouraged. How frustrating would that be?

Then, suddenly, you know *exactly* where the hoop is, and you have a clear purpose in mind: get that ball in the basket! Now the game becomes much more exciting and fulfilling. You know what you need to do, and you're focused on achieving that goal. Even if you miss a few shots, you're still driven by your purpose, and you'll keep going until you score that point.

The same is true in life. Without purpose, we're just wandering aimlessly, not really sure what we're supposed to be doing. But when we know what we want to achieve, we can lock in and get focused on making it happen.

## Finding your purpose

So, how do you find your purpose? Well, ultimately, that's a question only you can answer. The Purposeek Coaching Method isn't about finding your purpose *for* you, but rather empowering you to discover it for yourself.

According to Aristotle, our purpose is not merely to achieve happiness but to cultivate it through the continuous development of our highest self. He believed that true happiness, or what he called *eudaimonia*, is found in the realisation of our full potential and living a life of purpose and excellence. This means engaging in activities and pursuits that enhance our virtues, foster personal growth, and contribute to the well-being of society. By striving to improve ourselves and live virtuously, we achieve a deeper, more enduring form of happiness that aligns with our intrinsic nature and ultimate purpose.

'Wait a minute,' you might be saying now, 'I thought I was reading this book to get advice on switching jobs, not reach some higher state of being!' The fact is, though, that the feelings and motivations that are driving us towards considering a career change are intrinsically linked to those deeper and more profound aspects of our character. All of us feel as if there is else inside us that we haven't been able to show yet, some strength or ability we haven't had a chance to bring out. And career change is one of the many means of expressing and utilising that untapped potential.

So, before we get back to the subject of career change, I want you to read the questions in the following exercise, reflect on them, and write down your answers in the space below:

## DISCOVERING YOUR PURPOSE

Think about what makes you happy. What activities do you enjoy? What brings you the most satisfaction?

- Consider your values. What's most important to you? What do you stand for?

  _____

  _____

- Reflect on your strengths. What are you good at? What comes naturally to you?

  _____

  _____

- How can you make a difference in the world? How can you use your talents and skills to help others?

  _____

  _____

We're going to dig back into these questions, and your answers to them, later in the book. But remember, just like the previous exercises you've done, what you've written down above is a work in progress, not a one-time-only event. As your career-change journey progresses, you'll find yourself returning to these core questions again and again, refining and sometimes refocusing your answers to them through a regular process of self-reflection, experimentation, self-discovery and even, sometimes, (productive) failure.

But at this point, we're going to put something down in black and white to give you a clear direction in the immediate present. Let's start to define your purpose statement.

## Crafting your purpose statement

A purpose statement is a concise declaration that captures the essence of your personal mission, the reason for your existence, and the impact you want to make in the world.

Think of your purpose statement as a guiding light that illuminates your path and provides clarity and direction. It serves as a compass, helping you make decisions, set goals, and align your actions with your core values and aspirations. A well-crafted purpose statement encapsulates your unique gifts, passions and values, and defines the overarching purpose that drives your life.

However, your purpose statement is not a static declaration set in stone. It's a dynamic expression of your evolving self, capable of adapting and expanding as you grow and gain new experiences. It reflects your authentic self and can serve as a source of inspiration, motivation and resilience during both the highs and lows of your journey.

In the previous chapters, I guided you through a detailed process to examine your past, present and future, as well as your values, passions, desires and needs. The clarity and self-knowledge you gained through those exercises will now assist you in uncovering the core elements that make up your purpose. You are now well equipped to create an expression of the most authentic version of yourself.

Before we dive into the exercise, let me introduce you to the concept of Neuro-Linguistic Programming, or NLP. NLP is a psychological approach that involves analysing the strategies used by successful individuals and applying them to reach personal goals. It focuses on the connection between neurological processes, language and behavioural patterns learned through experience. In the context of this exercise, NLP will help you visualise and articulate your purpose by aligning your thoughts, emotions and actions.

Now, find a calm and relaxed spot, and follow the steps below.

## NLP VISUALISATION TO DEFINE YOUR PURPOSE STATEMENT

### STEP 1: VISUALISE YOUR STRENGTHS

Close your eyes and breathe slowly in and out, four to six times. Then, visualise a moment at work when you were strong, had a great success, or were powerful. Remember how it felt, through all your senses.

Now, open your eyes, and in the space below write out all the strengths you demonstrated in that moment, until you can't think of any more.

_____

_____

_____

### STEP 2: VISUALISE YOUR RECOGNITION

Close your eyes again and imagine people in the street, walking. Everyone has the same newspaper and is reading it very carefully, with smiles on their faces. You come closer, and realise there is a massive picture of you on the front page.

What does the headline above your photo say? When you've visualised it in your head, open your eyes and write it down below (and maybe even the sub-headline, too!).

_____

_____

_____

## STEP 3: VISUALISE YOUR METAPHOR

Close your eyes one more time, and think of an object or a living creature that best represents you—something that embodies all your strengths, and the ideal version of you that you want to become. Once you have it in your head, open your eyes and write (or draw) the metaphor of yourself below.

_____

_____

_____

What do these three exercises above have to do with creating your purpose statement? Precisely this:

- Your **strengths** reveal the core qualities that define who you are at your best, providing insight into what you naturally excel at and what brings you a sense of accomplishment.

- The **headline** reflects how you want to be seen and recognised by the world, encapsulating the impact you wish to make and the legacy you want to leave.

- Finally, the **metaphor** serves as a powerful symbol of your essence, capturing the unique combination of attributes that make you, you.

By bringing these elements together, you can distil them into a clear, concise purpose statement that encapsulates your mission, your vision, and the core values that drive you.

This statement will serve as your guiding star, helping you stay aligned with your true self as you navigate your career change and beyond.

Your purpose statement can follow a formula like this: 'I am [*your name*], because I love [*your passions*] and I want to [*your impact*].' But it can also take whatever form you like—this is *your* purpose, after all, so it should reflect exactly who *you* are! And remember, this is for your eyes only, so take your time to write and rewrite it as much as you want, until you feel it makes sense to you.

Purpose Statement:

_____

_____

_____

_____

## Conclusion

Crafting your purpose statement is not just an exercise—it's a pivotal moment in your journey of self-discovery and career transformation. This statement serves as the foundation for everything that follows, providing clarity and direction as you move forward.

As we move into the next chapters, this purpose statement will be your compass, helping you navigate the complexities of your career change with a clear sense of who you are and what you stand for. It will anchor you in moments of uncertainty and propel you towards opportunities that resonate with your authentic self. With your purpose statement defined, you're now ready to take the next steps in your journey, turning your vision into reality and making meaningful progress towards the life and career you desire.

# Chapter 9

# Translate Your Findings to Your Reality

AT LAST, HERE'S the chapter you've been waiting for—the one where we take the purpose statement you've crafted, and use it to implement a structure with which we can overcome (what often seems like) the chaos of career change.

I'm sure there are some readers out there who think that the book should have started with this chapter! But the fact is, even if it did, the results would not be the same. All the great work you've done to this point was meant to equip you with a deeper understanding of your true self, so that you can undertake your career-change journey with focus and purpose. Now, having explored and defined your values, passions, motivations, and what makes you reach your state of flow, you're prepared to ideate a career path that could be the jackpot for you.

But before we get started, I want you to gather together the three foundational exercises you've completed so far:

- Your answer to 'Who do you think you are?' (the latest version)

- Your mind map

- Your purpose statement

Assemble these three exercises in front of you and consider them side by side. Are they aligned with each other, or are there any tweaks required to make them match up? If so, take a few minutes to play around with them until they make sense to you as a cohesive whole; feel free to go back and perform one or more of the exercises again if you feel like it's necessary. Don't worry, I'll still be here when you get back!

All done? Great! Now that you have your three key elements lined up, it's time for me to share one of the most amazing tools I've used in my consulting career and in designing the Purposeek Coaching program: design thinking.

## Applying design thinking to your career-change journey

Design thinking is a creative, human-centred method for solving problems that was inspired by the late education and innovation thought leader Sir Ken Robinson. It consists of five stages:

1 **Empathise**: understand the needs, desires and challenges of those you are designing for, including yourself.

2 **Define**: synthesise information to frame the core problem you want to address.

3 **Ideate**: brainstorm a wide range of creative ideas and potential solutions.

4 **Prototype**: create tangible representations of your ideas.

5 **Test**: gather feedback and validate the solutions.

We're going to go through each of these stages step by step to begin charting your ideal career path. If you have questions, call a friend for support and feedback and do the exercise together.

**Empathise**

Empathy is often defined as 'slipping into someone else's shoes' and understanding their thoughts and emotions from the inside. In this instance, that someone else is actually you! What we're going to do here is look at you as if you're outside yourself, and closely examine the three key elements we revisited at the beginning of this chapter—your mind map, purpose statement, and declaration of 'who you think you are'. Then we'll complete the following exercise based on the person you see.

## VISUALISING YOUR PURPLE PURPOSE CAREER

- Recall the skills, passions and interests you identified in previous exercises. Spend a few minutes reflecting deeply one what energises you and what would give you fulfilment in an ideal career. Write down your answers below.

- Imagine if you could design your dream career from scratch—what would it be? Write down your ideal job title.

- Imagine encouraging yourself as you would a friend who was exploring this new career path, using kind, supportive words. Write down your advice below.

- List the skills you have or want to develop for your ideal career.

- Picture your future self in this ideal career. How does it align with your long-term goals and values?

- Reflect on how this ideal career might impact your well-being, happiness and work-life balance. Write down your insights.

### Define

In the second stage of our design-thinking model, we're going to draw on the insights you wrote down in the 'empathy' exercise above and synthesise that information to identify some specific challenges and obstacles involved in pursuing your ideal career path. By defining potential problems, we can then go about making more-informed decisions and developing strategies for how to deal with them.

## DEFINING YOUR PURPLE PURPOSE CAREER

- Write down a detailed description of your ideal job. What are your responsibilities? What kind of environment are you in? What impact are you making?

  _____

  _____

- List potential challenges or obstacles that may arise in achieving this ideal job. Consider both internal factors (e.g. skill gaps) and external factors (e.g. industry trends or job market conditions). For the latter, you can draw on the work you did in Chapter 7.

  _____

  _____

- From your list of challenges, identify the core problems you need to address—that is, the main obstacles standing between you and your ideal job.

  _____

  _____

## Ideate

In this stage, we will brainstorm a wide range of potential solutions for the core problems we identified above, not limiting ourselves to only conventional or expected ideas.

## DESIGNING YOUR PURPLE PURPOSE CAREER—STEP 1:

- Grab a large sheet of paper or use a digital mind mapping tool, whichever you prefer.

- Write down your ideal job at the centre of the mind map. Brainstorm various career possibilities that align with your ideal job. Set a timer for fifteen or twenty minutes and list potential career roles that match your skills, interests and values, considering various industries, job titles or entrepreneurial ventures.

- Draw branches connecting each career possibility to your career aspiration in the centre of your map. (Now's the time to go back to the preliminary action plan you completed in the 'Passions' section of Chapter 4, and incorporate those potential career paths in your map.)

- For each potential career opportunity, create a web of sub-branches, listing related skills, qualifications, or aspects of the job that catch your interest.

- Use different colours, icons or images to highlight aspects of each career opportunity that resonate with you.

- Look for connections between your various career options— e.g. industries that might require similar skill sets or share common values.

Below is a diagram illustrating the above exercise, using the career option of 'travel blogger':

## Designing Your Purple Purpose Career

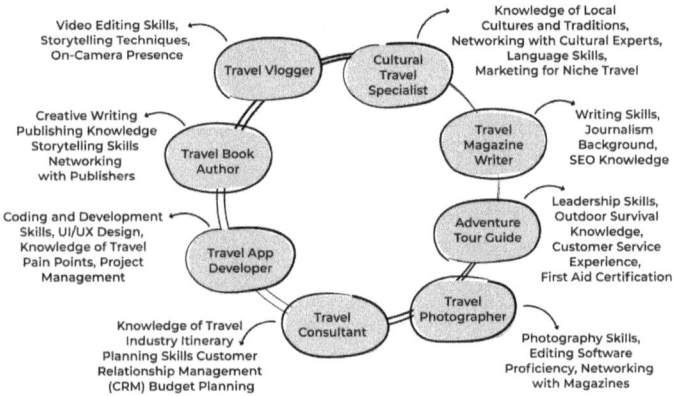

To guide you in creating your own diagram, start by listing your potential career options. For each option, outline the required skills and qualifications, similar to the following example provided below:

Travel Blogger:
Travel vlogger, Travel photographer, Travel magazine writer, Adventure tour guide, Travel consultant, Travel influencer Travel app developer, Travel book author, Cultural travel specialist, Sustainable travel advocate

Skills and Qualifications:

Travel Vlogger
- Video editing skills
- Storytelling techniques
- On-camera presence
- YouTube platform knowledge

Travel Photographer
- Photography skills
- Editing software proficiency

## STEP 2

Analyse your skills, qualifications and interests to narrow down your potential career options to three. I also recommend taking a step back to review your mind map, as it can help with your analysis and shortlisting process.

The diagram below illustrates the process of narrowing down career options based on skills, qualifications and interests, leading to the top three career choices:

- Travel blogger
- Travel photographer
- Travel consultant

## Top 3 career choices

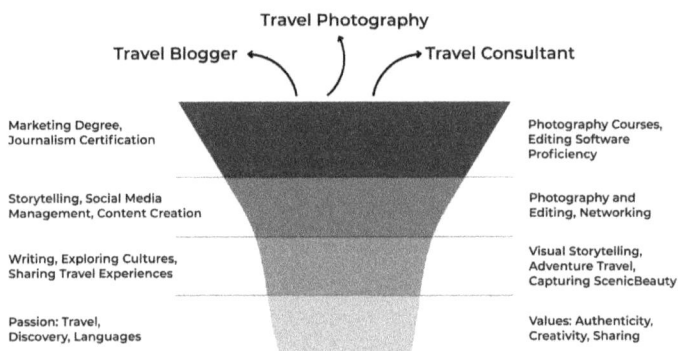

Travel Photography

Travel Blogger → ← → Travel Consultant

Marketing Degree,
Journalism Certification

Photography Courses,
Editing Software
Proficiency

Storytelling, Social Media
Management, Content Creation

Photography and
Editing, Networking

Writing, Exploring Cultures,
Sharing Travel Experiences

Visual Storytelling,
Adventure Travel,
Capturing ScenicBeauty

Passion: Travel,
Discovery, Languages

Values: Authenticity,
Creativity, Sharing

## STEP 3

Once you've identified your top three career options, use the ranking process to determine the best fit. In the table below, list, score and rank each career option across the following categories, using a scale of 1 to 10 for each:

- Interest
- Values alignment
- Financial benefits
- Positive impact
- Potential for growth
- Gut feeling

Here's the scoring table using the 'travel blogger' example:

| Career Opportunities | Travel Blogger | Travel Photographer | Travel Consultant |
|---|---|---|---|
| Interest | 9 | 8 | 7 |
| Value Alignment | 9 | 7 | 8 |
| Financial Benefits | 7 | 6 | 8 |
| Positive Impact | 8 | 7 | 6 |
| Gut Feeling | 8 | 8 | 9 |
| Potential for Growth | 9 | 7 | 8 |
| Average score | 8.3 | 7.2 | 7.7 |

| Career Opportunities | Career 1 Score (1 to 10) | Career 2 Score (1 to 10) | Career... Score (1 to 10) |
|---|---|---|---|
| Interest | | | |
| Values alignment | | | |
| Financial benefits | | | |
| Positive Impact | | | |
| Potential for growth | | | |
| Gut feeling | | | |
| Average score | | | |

Tally your scores from the table above and, based on the results, write down your top career opportunity below (i.e. the career with the highest total score):

_____

_____

_____

_____

_____

_____

_____

## Prototype

At this stage we are going to further visualise and clarify your career options, ensuring that your choices are based on a well-rounded understanding of each potential path. To accomplish this, we will use two exercises: a SWOT career analysis, and discovery interviews.

### SWOT analysis

The **SWOT analysis**—which stands for 'Strengths', 'Weaknesses', 'Opportunities' and 'Threats'—provides a structured way to visualise and evaluate your career options against both internal and external factors, allowing you to assess which career paths are most viable and aligned with your capabilities.

## PROTOTYPING YOUR PURPLE PURPOSE CAREER: SWOT CAREER ANALYSIS

- Create a table divided into four quadrants: Strengths, Weaknesses, Opportunities and Threats.

---

- Write down your top three career options under the Opportunities quadrant.

---

- List your skills and qualities under the Strengths and Weaknesses quadrants.

---

- Note down any challenges or obstacles you might face under the Threats quadrant.

---

Here's an example of a SWOT table, with the potential career paths 'marketing manager', 'life coach' and our old friend, 'travel blogger':

| Strengths | Weaknesses | Opportunities | Threats |
|---|---|---|---|
| Good Communication Skills | Limited Technical Skills | Career 1: Marketing Manager | High Competition |
| Strong Leadership | Lack of Industry Experience | Career 2: Travel Blogger | Financial Instability |
| Creativity and Innovation | Need for Additional Training | Career 3: Life Coach | Certification Requirements |

Discovery interviews

A **discovery interview** is a more labour-intensive exercise, so don't worry about completing it right now—you can move on through the rest of the book first. But I wanted to include this here because it's the ideal complement to the SWOT analysis you completed above.

By reaching out to and speaking directly with professionals in the fields you've identified as your potential career paths, you gain valuable insights that can't be found in job descriptions or career guides. This firsthand information will help you understand the day-to-day realities of your chosen careers and evaluate whether they truly match your interests and skills.

The steps to complete for your discovery interviews are:

- Connect with individuals currently working in your chosen fields.

- Schedule interviews to learn about their career paths, experiences and insights.

- Seek guidance on breaking into the industry and the skills that are most valuable.

- Reflect on the information gathered and assess how it aligns with your goals and aspirations.

## Test

In this phase, we'll test your top three potential career options out in the real world, as sometimes what looks good on paper might not feel right in practice. This test will cover three distinct phases:

## JOB SHADOWING

Spend a day or more shadowing someone in each of your top three fields to gain firsthand experience of the real-world career environment. By shadowing professionals, you gain firsthand experience and insights into the daily responsibilities, challenges and rewards of each field.

## SIDE PROJECT/VOLUNTEER OPPORTUNITY

Engage in a side project or volunteer work related to your top career options to test your interest and skills. This hands-on experience tests your abilities and commitment, providing a clearer picture of what it takes to succeed in these roles.

For example, if you are considering a career in digital marketing, a potential side project could be starting a blog or managing social media accounts for a small business or non-profit organisation. This would allow you to develop and showcase your content creation, SEO and analytics skills. Alternatively, volunteering to help with marketing efforts for a local charity could give you experience in campaign management and community outreach, helping you decide if this path truly aligns with your strengths and passions.

## OBSERVE AND REFLECT

Based on your experiences in the exercises above, evaluate how well each career option fits your personal and professional goals.

## Determine your preferred career opportunity

Once you have conducted the SWOT analysis, discovery interviews and job shadowing, revisit the career path you chose in the ideate phase. Now, ask yourself the key question:

*Is this still the career you prefer? Does it genuinely excite you, align with your values, and support your long-term goals? Or, upon reflection, does another option among your top three choices seem like a better fit?*

Take time to consider this carefully, and when you're ready, write down your top choice in the space that follows.

Preferred career opportunity:

## Conclusion

As you ponder that big question above, remember that clarity often comes from action. As you continue this journey of self-discovery and exploration, the next chapter will guide you through the critical process of working on your mindset. This is an essential step in preparing yourself mentally and emotionally for the career transition ahead. Once your mindset is in the right place, you'll be ready to create a concrete plan for your career transition.

# Chapter 10

# Your Mindset—
# Your Success!

AFTER COMPLETING THE work in the last chapter, you should be feeling like you have a lot more clarity about what you want to do and where you want to go. However, even with that accomplishment under your belt, it's not at all surprising if those old feelings of fear and self-doubt are making an unwelcome return.

But don't worry! It's completely normal to experience a mix of excitement and apprehension when faced with a new challenge. And even if the latter has the edge at the moment, we can help tame those fears by applying two 'Ps' from the Purposeek Coaching Method: Perspective and Prosperity.

Why are we addressing these two Ps together? Because they are inseparable and synergistic, and work on the most important asset you have: your mindset. In this chapter, we are going to cover exercises that will help you conquer your fears, overcome your limiting beliefs, and cultivate a resilient mindset that will help propel you forward on your career-change journey, equipped with the mental strength and fortitude needed to tackle any obstacles that may arise along the way.

## Managing your fears

We all know the famous expression 'No pain, no gain'. But allow me to introduce a little twist on that old maxim: 'No *fear*, no gain'.

The fact is, even when you know where your true purpose lies and what you have to do to get there, fear will be your companion along the way. And, all too often, we take this fear as a sign that we need to stop, or even turn back completely. In reality, however, that fear is a sign that we are on the right track and must keep going, pushing through the discomfort.

Your fears won't vanish as you embark on your transformative journey. They might come and go, sometimes be under control, and at other times feel overwhelming. The trick is to accept this reality, and learn how to manage (not vanquish) those feelings of doubt and apprehension.

The first step in that process is to pin down just what it is that makes you feel so afraid of the ideal career that you've charted for yourself. In the exercise below, we'll take a step-by-step approach to identify and assess the major fear that is holding you back; as with the exercise in the previous chapter, I've included some example answers to give you an idea of what you should be aiming for in your own replies.

## TRANSFORMING YOUR FEARS INTO STRENGTHS

- Identify a specific fear that is holding you back. Write it down below, with as much detail as you can. (e.g. 'I am afraid of public speaking.')

  _____

  _____

- Reflect on the origin of this fear. Ask yourself, 'Why do I feel this way? What past experiences or beliefs are contributing to this fear?' (e.g. 'I am afraid of public speaking because I had a bad experience in school where I forgot my speech and everyone laughed.')

  _____

  _____

- Evaluate the validity of this fear. Is it based on facts or assumptions? Look for evidence that contradicts it.

  _____

  _____

- Turn your fear into a positive statement. (e.g. if your fear is 'I am afraid of failing,' reframe it as 'Failure is an opportunity to learn and grow.')

  _____

  _____

- Develop a step-by-step plan to address your fear. Break down the steps into manageable actions that will help you gradually face and overcome the fear.

  _____

  _____

- Start implementing your plan. Take small steps towards confronting your fear and celebrate each success, no matter how small.

  _____

  _____

- Regularly reflect on your progress. Adjust your plan as needed, and continue taking steps forward.

  _____

  _____

- Share your fear and plan with a trusted friend, mentor, or coach. Having someone to support and encourage you can make a significant difference.

  _____

  _____

This exercise is designed to help you confront and manage the fears that may be holding you back in your career and life. By identifying, understanding and reframing your fears, you'll be able to turn them into stepping stones to growth and success.

## The empowering rewrite: Overcoming your self-doubts and limiting beliefs

One often hears the popular phrase: 'Believe in yourself, and all your dreams will manifest.' But is it easy to truly feel and embody that belief? From my own experiences, and those of my clients, I'd say that the answer is often no. No matter how often you repeat positive affirmations to yourself, unhelpful thoughts like 'I'm not good enough', 'I can't do it' or 'This is too hard' can weigh heavily on your mind, making it difficult to move forward.

However, the good news is that, unlike fears, self-doubt and limiting beliefs *can* be overcome, not just managed. There are various techniques for accomplishing this, but one approach that I find particularly empowering is to rewrite and create your own narrative.

## TRANSFORMING LIMITING BELIEFS INTO EMPOWERING TRUTHS

- Begin by identifying one or two specific limiting beliefs that are holding you back or causing self-doubt.

- Take a moment to question the validity and accuracy of the limiting belief. Ask yourself, 'Is this belief based on facts, or is it a self-imposed limitation?'

- Reframe the limiting belief as an empowering and supportive statement.

- Reinforce your new empowering belief by gathering evidence that supports it. Recall past achievements, moments of personal growth, and positive feedback you have received.

- Craft positive affirmations that align with your new narrative. Repeat these affirmations daily, both in your mind and out loud, to reinforce the positive beliefs.

- Take time each day to visualise yourself embodying your new narrative. Create vivid mental images of yourself succeeding, overcoming challenges, and living the life you desire. Engage all your senses to make the visualisation more powerful and compelling.

- Regularly revisit your new narrative and affirmations. Read them aloud, reflect on their meaning and internalise them. Consistency is key in rewiring your mindset and replacing limiting beliefs with empowering ones.

- Reach out to a trusted friend, mentor or coach to share your new narrative and receive encouragement and accountability. Having someone who can provide support and remind you of your worth can make the process even more transformative.

Changing your narrative takes time and effort. Be patient and compassionate with yourself as you work through this exercise, and commit each day to embracing your new beliefs and taking steps towards a more empowering and fulfilling life.

## Cultivate the power of positive thinking

Overcoming our internal obstacles is crucial, but equally important is to build strong, positive new mental structures in their place. This begins with understanding the power of positive thoughts, and how they can change our perspective and drive us towards the right path.

Positive thinking is more than just a mood booster—it's a crucial component of mental resilience and success. When we adopt a positive mindset, we open ourselves up to new possibilities, attract positive outcomes and foster a more fulfilling life. Some of the benefits include:

- **Enhanced problem-solving skills**. Positive thinking enhances your ability to think creatively and solve problems. When you're optimistic, you're more likely to see solutions rather than obstacles.

- **Better health**. Numerous studies have shown that positive thinking can improve physical health and reduce stress.

- **Increased resilience**. A positive mindset helps you bounce back from setbacks more quickly. You're more likely to view failures as opportunities to learn and grow.

- **Improved relationships**. Positivity attracts positivity. When you exude a positive attitude, you're more likely to build strong, supportive relationships.

- **Greater success**. Positive thinkers are more motivated, persistent and likely to achieve their goals. They believe in their abilities and take proactive steps to make their dreams a reality.

A simple yet powerful daily exercise to help you cultivate a positive mindset is to start keeping a gratitude journal.

## GRATITUDE JOURNALING

- Take your journal and a pen, and sit down in a quiet place where you won't be disturbed.

- Take a few moments to think about your day. What went well? What made you smile? What are you thankful for?

- Write down at least three positive things that happened that day. They don't have to be big events—small moments of joy or gratitude count too. For example: 'I had a delicious cup of coffee', 'I completed a challenging task at work' or 'I enjoyed a nice walk in the park'.

- When noting down larger things that you're grateful for, try to be as specific as possible. For example, instead of writing 'I'm grateful for my family', try 'I'm grateful for my sister's encouraging words during our phone call'.

- After writing, take a moment to reflect on each entry. Relive the positive feelings associated with each moment.

Make your gratitude journal a daily habit. Over time, you'll train your mind to focus on the positive aspects of your life, fostering a more optimistic outlook.

### Embracing a growth mindset

'Growth mindset' is a concept that was popularised by Carol Dweck in *Mindset: Changing the Way you Think to Fulfil your Potential*, which is a book that transformed my perspective on both my life and my career. I used to dread and avoid hardship and eagerly wait for or seek out ease, but after reading this book I came to recognise the value in hardship itself and to see that every experience, whether positive or negative, is an opportunity for growth. In this context, setbacks become valuable teachers: they provide insights and guide us in the right direction.

Adopting a growth mindset allows us to:

- **Embrace challenges**. View challenges as opportunities to learn and grow.

- **Persist in the face of setbacks**. Understand that setbacks are part of the journey and use them as learning experiences.

- **See effort as the path to mastery**. Recognise that effort and hard work are essential for developing skills and achieving success.

- **Learn from criticism**. Use feedback as a tool for improvement rather than taking it personally.

- **Find inspiration in others' success**. Instead of feeling threatened by others' success, use it as motivation to improve yourself.

By developing a growth mindset, we open ourselves to continuous improvement and resilience. We begin to understand that every setback, every struggle, is a stepping stone towards becoming a stronger, more resilient version of ourselves. As the champion MMA fighter Khabib Nurmagomedov wisely said, 'God gives hardship to those who He loves, so I take it as an honour.'

In the exercise below, we're going to practise cultivating this kind of resilience.

## EMBRACING HARDSHIP
## AND CELEBRATING EFFORT

- Think of a recent hardship or challenge you faced, either at work or in your personal life. Write down a brief description of the situation and how it made you feel.

  _____

  _____

- Ask yourself, 'What did I learn from this experience?' Identify at least one lesson or positive takeaway from the challenge and write it down.

  _____

  _____

- Consider the effort you put into facing this challenge, regardless of the outcome. Write down the actions you took, the energy you invested, and what you can be proud of. Celebrate the fact that you took on the challenge, even if things didn't go perfectly.

  _____

  _____

- Based on what you learned, set a simple goal or intention for how you will approach similar challenges in the future. For example, 'Next time, I will focus on staying calm and asking for help when needed.'

  _____

  _____

## Conclusion

In this chapter, you've learned that your mindset isn't just an abstract concept—it's a powerful tool that can shape your reality, influence your actions, and determine the outcome of your career-change journey. By embracing a growth mindset, reframing your fears and reinforcing empowering beliefs, you've laid the foundation for resilience and continuous improvement.

Your mindset is the lens through which you view your challenges, opportunities and potential. As you've seen, adopting a growth mindset allows you to perceive setbacks as learning experiences, to celebrate effort alongside achievement, and to approach every obstacle with confidence and curiosity. This mindset will not only help you navigate the uncertainties of a career change, but also empower you to thrive in any future endeavour.

As you move forward, remember that the work on your mindset is ongoing. The tools and exercises you've explored in this chapter are meant to be revisited, refined and integrated into your daily life. By doing so, you'll continue to strengthen the mental and emotional resilience needed to achieve your goals.

In the next chapter, we'll take the insights and mental fortitude you've developed here and apply them to creating a concrete plan for your career transition. It's time to turn your newfound clarity and confidence into decisive, purposeful action.

# Chapter 11

# Take Action

SO FAR IN this book, we've undertaken a journey of self-discovery to learn more about our purpose, harnessed the power of design thinking to translate that purpose into a plan for our life and career, and rewired our minds to help us manage our fears and limiting beliefs about the path ahead. Now it's time to grab life by the horns and make things happen!

In this chapter, we're going to learn how to transform our goals into concrete steps and purposeful actions so that we can make our dreams into our reality. In the exercises below, you will discover some foundational principles that will empower you to move forward with clarity, intention and unwavering focus. Whether you aspire to land your dream job, start a passion-driven business, or embark on some other adventurous new path, this formula will guide you every step of the way.

## From vision to action: Crafting your roadmap

### Step 1: Set the stage
*Goals are the fuel that propels us towards greatness.*

Take a piece of paper and a pen. Write down your vision in the centre of the page, and list the goals associated with that vision in a cloud around it.

For example, if your vision is 'start a sustainable fashion brand', the associated goals could be, i) researching sustainable materials and suppliers, ii) developing a brand identity and logo, iii) creating a business plan, and so on.

### Step 2: Get tactical
*Plans without action are just daydreams.*

Break your goals down into manageable steps to create an action plan. Each task should be measurable and attainable, but also exciting enough to get your heart pumping. Write down a few initial thoughts below.

## Step 3: Dive in

*The biggest leap starts with a single step.*

Review the tasks you've identified, and commit to undertaking the one that excites you the most and/or makes you the most nervous. This first courageous leap will give you the momentum you need to keep you going.

## Step 4: Unleash the warrior within

*Discipline turns dreams into reality.*

Cultivate discipline, by creating daily habits and routines that align with your goals. Small actions, performed consistently, have the power to move mountains.

For example, you could commit to sustaining a daily exercise routine and nourishing your body with wholesome foods.

### Step 5: Rally the troops

*Alone, we can do so little; together, we can do so much.*

Seek support and accountability from your tribe. Share your goals with trusted friends, mentors or an online community. Their encouragement and guidance will keep you motivated and accountable.

### Step 6: Break out the confetti

*Celebrate every tiny victory as if it were a grand triumph!*

Pause to celebrate your wins, big or small. Treat yourself to something joyful, throw a party, or simply revel in your progress. Life's too short to *not* celebrate!

### Step 7: Reflect, iterate and conquer

*Success is a journey, not a destination.*

Reflect on your actions, learn from your experiences, and refine your approach. Be open to new insights, feedback and unexpected twists. This ongoing reflection is key to continuous improvement and long-term success.

## Devising your career action plan

We're almost at the finish line! Stay focused and purposeful as we undertake this last exercise, which is to devise an action plan for your ideal career. (You can refer to the preferred career opportunity that you jotted down at the end of Chapter 9.)

## CAREER ACTION PLAN

- Outline the steps required to transition to your preferred career.

- Break down the process of changing careers into smaller, actionable steps.

- Create specific tasks and milestones to accomplish for each, and set deadlines.

- Identify resources and support systems you may need to accomplish each task.

- Maintain a journal to document your experiences and seek feedback.

In 3rd action in above list suggest: Create specific tasks, adding milestones needed to accomplish them, and set deadlines. I've included an example of a completed career action plan below, with an 'entirely random' ideal career path.

# IDEAL CAREER:
# LIFE AND CAREER COACH

| Activity | Milestone | Deadline | Resources/ Support |
|---|---|---|---|
| Research training programs | Research various life and career coach training programs | Complete research within two weeks | Online resources, coaching associations, recommendations |
| Enrol in coaching certification program | Choose and enrol in a reputable coaching certification program | Start the program within one month | Coaching program advisors, enrolment assistance |
| Build coaching skills | Attend coaching workshops and practice coaching sessions | Engage in workshops and sessions within four months | Coaching mentors, practice partners, feedback |
| Create coaching portfolio | Develop a portfolio showcasing your coaching expertise | Complete portfolio within six months | Peer reviews, coaching mentors |
| Establish online presence | Create a professional website and social media profiles | Establish online presence within eight months | Web developers, online branding guides |
| Network and acquire clients | Attend coaching events and connect with potential clients | Begin networking and client acquisition within ten months | Coaching communities, networking events |
| Offer pro bono coaching | Provide pro bono coaching to gain experience and testimonials | Start offering pro bono coaching within 12 months | Non-profit organisations, mentor guidance |
| Develop coaching packages and pricing | Create coaching packages and set pricing | Establish packages and pricing within fourteen months | Business coaches, industry benchmarks |

| Activity | Milestone | Deadline | Resources/ Support |
|---|---|---|---|
| Launch coaching business | Officially launch your coaching business | Launch within sixteen months | Business mentors, legal advice |
| Start a podcast | Launch a podcast to share insights and build your brand | Launch podcast within six months | Podcast hosting platforms, recording equipment, marketing strategies |
| Develop digital coaching products | Create and sell online courses and e-books to reach a wider audience | Develop and launch digital products within eight months | e-learning platforms, content creation tools, marketing plans |
| Write a book | Author a book to share your expertise | Complete and publish the book within twelve months | Writing coaches, publishers, editors |
| Continue professional development | Engage in ongoing learning and development as a coach | Ongoing! | Coaching conferences, workshops, coaching associations |

As you've seen, the example career path I selected was not so random at all, was it? These are some of the actual action plans I developed as I was engineering my own career transition. And, true confession: I missed all the deadlines I set for myself. (For example, it ended up taking me four years to write my book, instead of the planned twelve months!)

However, as I continued to push towards my goal, I realised that life doesn't always unfold according to our expectations. One of the biggest lessons I learned from this process was the importance of flexibility and adaptability. Instead of rigidly sticking to my original plan, I allowed myself to explore new opportunities as they arose. This openness led to unexpected collaborations, new learning experiences, and a coaching program that evolved far beyond what I had initially envisioned.

The result? A more dynamic and impactful coaching practice than I could ever have planned for!

## Conclusion

As we end this chapter, it's crucial to recognise that all the self-discovery, planning and mindset work we've done thus far culminates in one essential truth: action is the catalyst that turns dreams into reality. You can have the clearest vision, the most detailed plan and the strongest mindset, but without action, these remain merely potential.

Taking action is where the magic happens. It's where ideas transform into tangible outcomes, where plans are tested and refined, and where progress is made. It's through action that you build momentum, gain confidence, and learn the lessons that only experience can teach.

Remember, the journey towards your purpose-driven career isn't about perfection—it's about progress. Every step you take, no matter how small, brings you closer to the life and career you envision. So, take that first step, and then the next, and the next. Embrace the power of action as your ally in this journey.

As you move forward, keep in mind that action is not a one-time event but a continuous commitment to your goals. There will be challenges, but with every challenge comes an opportunity to learn, grow, and adjust your course as needed.

In the next chapter, we'll explore how to translate your actions into sustainable habits and practices that will keep you moving steadily towards your goals. But for now, let's celebrate the fact that you're ready to take charge of your journey and make things happen.

# Chapter 12

# Turning Actions into Sustainable Habits

AT THIS POINT in your career-change journey, you've outlined your goals, developed a plan, and taken action. Now it's time to ensure that your momentum doesn't flag. The key to long-term success lies in your ability to transform these initial actions into sustainable habits and practices that will keep you moving steadily towards your goals.

Habits are the building blocks of our daily lives. They shape our actions, define our routines, and ultimately determine the trajectory of our personal and professional growth. When you establish positive, goal-oriented habits, you create a foundation that supports continuous progress, even when motivation fluctuates. Habits are the silent drivers of sustained success.

A study conducted by researchers at Duke University shows that approximately 40% of our daily actions are driven by habits rather than conscious decision-making.[8] This means that if you can build the right habits, you can significantly enhance your ability to achieve your goals without having to constantly rely on willpower or motivation alone.

---

8   Wood, W. & Neal, D. T. (2007). 'A new look at habits and the habit-goal interface'. *Psychological Review, 114*(4), 843–863. https://doi.org/10.1037/0033-295x.114.4.843

To effectively create sustainable habits, it's important to understand how habits work. According to Charles Duhigg, author of *The Power of Habit*, every habit consists of three components:

1 **Cue**: the trigger that initiates the habit. It could be a time of day, an emotional state, or an environmental factor

2 **Routine**: the behaviour or action that you perform in response to the cue

3 **Reward**: the positive reinforcement you receive after completing the routine, which encourages the habit to continue

For example, if you want to develop a habit of exercising every morning, your cue might be waking up and seeing your workout clothes laid out; your routine is completing your workout; and the reward could be the sense of accomplishment and energy boost you feel afterwards.

## Building sustainable habits

Now that you understand the structure of a habit, let's explore how to build habits that will help you stay on track with your goals.

### Step 1: Start small

One of the biggest mistakes people make when trying to build new habits is attempting to do too much too soon. Instead, focus on small, manageable actions that you can consistently perform. For example, if your goal is to write a book, start by committing to writing for just 10 minutes a day. This small step will gradually build into a habit that can expand over time.

### Step 2: Identify your cues

Choose cues that will trigger your new habit. These cues should be consistent and easily integrated into your daily routine. For example, if you want to meditate daily, your cue could be to begin after brushing your teeth in the morning. By linking your habit to an existing routine, you increase the likelihood of it sticking.

### Step 3: Establish a routine

Define the specific action you want to take in response to your cue. Ensure that the routine is simple enough that you can do it even on your busiest days. The more straightforward the routine, the easier it will be to maintain.

### Step 4: Reward yourself

After completing your routine, reward yourself in a way that reinforces the habit. The reward doesn't have to be extravagant; it could be something as simple as enjoying a cup of coffee or taking a few minutes to relax. The key is to associate the routine with a positive outcome.

### Step 5: Track your progress

Monitoring your progress is crucial for staying motivated and accountable. Use a habit tracker, journal or app to record your daily habits. Seeing your progress visually can provide a powerful sense of achievement and encourage you to keep going.

### Step 6: Be patient and persistent

Building new habits takes time. Studies suggest that it takes an average of sixty-six days for a new behaviour to become automatic, although this process can range anywhere from eighteen to 254 days depending on such factors as the mindset of the individual and the complexity of the behaviour.[9] So don't get discouraged if you miss a day or two—what matters is staying consistent and getting back on track. The key is perseverance and repetition, so keep moving forward, and your new habit will gradually take root.

### Step 7: Work to break your bad habits

Just as important as building new habits is breaking old ones that no longer serve you. Some techniques to start doing this include:

- **Identifying the cue.** Determine what triggers the bad habit.

- **Replacing the routine.** Swap out the negative behaviour with a positive one. For example, if you tend to reach for junk food when stressed, try replacing it with a healthier snack or a quick walk.

- **Rewarding yourself differently.** Find a new reward that reinforces the positive behaviour you've substituted.

To integrate your new habits into a cohesive routine, try designing your ideal day. This involves mapping out how you'd like your day to flow, from morning to night, incorporating your habits into each part of the day. This practice not only helps you visualise your goals but also makes it easier to implement them consistently.

---

9   Research by Phillippa Lally and her team at University College London, published in the European Journal of Social Psychology, How long does it take to form a habit? | UCL News - UCL—University College London, How Long Does It Take to Form a New Behaviour? - Dr. Michelle Cleere, Time to form a habit: 21 days or 1 year, answers from science - Cognition Today.

# DESIGNING YOUR IDEAL DAY

Morning routine:
- What habits will you practice in the morning? (e.g. exercise, journaling, meditation)

_____

_____

- What time will you wake up, and what will be your first action?

_____

_____


Workday habits:
- How will you incorporate productive habits into your workday? (e.g. focused work sessions, regular breaks, healthy eating)

_____

_____

- How will you manage distractions and stay on task?

_____

_____


Evening routine:
- What habits will help you unwind and prepare for the next day? (e.g. reading, reflection, planning)

_____

_____

- What time will you go to bed, and how will you ensure a restful night?

_____

_____

Flexibility and adaptation:
- How will you adjust your routine when unexpected events arise?

_____

_____

- How will you maintain your habits when your schedule changes?

_____

_____

## Conclusion

Sustainable habits are the foundation of long-term success. By transforming your goals into daily actions, you create a pathway to achieving your purpose and living a fulfilling life.

However, as you work to build those habits, remember that consistency is more important than perfection. Life will inevitably throw curveballs, and there will be days when you fall short. The key is to stay committed, keep moving forward, and celebrate your progress along the way.

# Conclusion
## It's about the journey,
## not the destination

AS WE REACH the final chapter of (the beginning of!) your transformative career-change journey, let's take a moment to reflect on the essence of what we have set out to achieve— a life centred on purpose.

Throughout this book, we have delved into the depths of self-discovery, harnessed the magic of design thinking and nurtured a growth mindset. Now it's time to come full circle and understand that the pursuit of purpose—which I call 'Purposeek'—is the driving force that makes our life journey extraordinary, fulfilling and downright fun!

However, as you might have noticed while reading, the chapter in which we craft your purpose statement comes in the middle, rather than right at the beginning. Why is this the case?

First of all, this is because the activities you completed in the initial chapters —digging into your intrinsic motivations to discover your drivers and your true self—are key to unlocking your purpose. The work you did there gave you the perspective and self-revelations you needed to drill down and find what you *really* want to be doing with your life and career.

Secondly, it's important to remember that finding your purpose does not mean you have arrived at your final destination. Our purpose can evolve and morph as we ourselves grow, change and gain new perspectives. You need to live fully before you can discover your purpose, by which I mean experimenting with different things, trying various paths, going through hardships, losing, failing, and feeling the pressure. Be alert and learn from everything, because this will allow you to discover your authentic self and, therefore, your purpose. And also remember that your purpose-seeking journey is not all hardship and difficulties—it's also filled with moments of joy, feel-good times, and connections with your faith, your environment and the people around you.

All that said, because of its ever-changing nature, discovering your purpose can feel like searching for a ring in the sand: it's not something that happens overnight, and it requires the right tools to track it down. As I said at the very beginning of this book, the Purposeek Coaching Method is not some 'one-size-fits-all' solution for career change. Rather, it's a resource that can help you conduct your own unique journey towards your purpose, help you navigate uncertainties with confidence, keep you motivated during difficult times and lift your spirits when needed.

So in that spirit, as you embark on your fantastic, purpose-driven journey towards your ideal career, I want to offer you a quick recap of the core principles that will be your companions along the way.

## Embrace curiosity and learning

- Stay open-minded. Embrace new experiences and perspectives. Let curiosity drive you to explore, learn and grow.

- Commit to continuous learning. Seek opportunities for personal and professional development. Enrol in courses, attend workshops, and read books that inspire and challenge you.

## Practise gratitude and mindfulness

- Regularly write down things you are grateful for in a gratitude journal. This practice fosters a positive mindset and helps you appreciate the small joys in your journey.

- Incorporate mindfulness practices into your routine. Being present in the moment can reduce stress and enhance your overall well-being.

## Build a support network

- Surround yourself with positivity by engaging with individuals who inspire and uplift you. Their support can provide valuable encouragement and motivation.

- Identify and seek out mentors who can offer guidance, share their experiences, and provide insights as you navigate your path.

## Celebrate small wins

- Acknowledge your progress and celebrate every milestone, no matter how small. Recognising your achievements boosts confidence and reinforces your commitment to your goals.

- Reward yourself when you accomplish significant tasks. These can be simple pleasures that bring you joy and satisfaction.

## Maintain balance

- Prioritise self-care. Ensure you take care of your physical, emotional and mental well-being. Balance work with rest and recreation to prevent burnout.

- Establish clear boundaries between your work and personal life. This balance is crucial for sustained productivity and happiness.

## Reflect and adapt

- Periodically take stock of your progress and reflect on your journey. This helps you stay aligned with your purpose and make necessary adjustments.

- Be open to change and willing to adapt your plans as you grow and evolve. Embracing flexibility allows you to navigate unexpected challenges with grace.

As you progress through your transformative journey, I encourage you to take charge of your career change by making decisions that are true to your values and aspirations. Let your choices be informed by thorough research, due diligence, your gut feeling, and, of course, your Purple Purpose! Free yourself from the limitations that hold you back. Embrace the path that is uniquely yours.

You are the author of your story, and your Purple Purpose is the ink that brings it to life. No matter your circumstances, you hold the power to shape your destiny. Take ownership of your life, unleash your potential, and create the change needed to live your own version of happiness and success. Seize the opportunities that come your way and courageously venture into the unknown, guided by your purpose-seeking journey.

Now, you not only know you have what it takes to succeed, but you also have a method that will be your best friend and faithful companion during your career-change journey—one that will constantly remind you to stay true to your authentic self and take meaningful action towards your dream career.

As you embark on this exciting new chapter of your life, remember that the journey itself is filled with valuable lessons, growth and unforgettable experiences. Embrace every twist and turn with an open heart, and let your purpose guide you towards a life of fulfilment, meaning and joy.

Sending you lots of love, prayers and good vibes! Go out there and make your dreams a reality. You've got this!

With all my best wishes,

**MYRIEM SLATER**
Purposeful entrepreneur & founder
of the Purposeek Coaching Method

# Connect with Me

THANK YOU for reading this book and engaging with the principles of the Purposeek Coaching Method. If you've found value in these pages and are eager to take the next step in your career-change journey, I would love to continue supporting you.

For those who want further information or are interested in signing up for the Purposeek program, you can connect with me in the following ways:

**Website**: Visit www.purposeekcoaching.com.au to explore more about the Purposeek Coaching Method, access additional resources, and sign up for my coaching programs. The website offers a wealth of free content, insightful blog posts, and details about upcoming events and workshops.

**Email**: Feel free to reach out directly at myriem@purposeek coaching.com.au. Whether you have questions, need guidance, or want to discuss how the Purposeek Coaching Method can help you, I'm here to support you.

**LinkedIn**: Connect with me on LinkedIn at www.linkedin. com/in/myriem-slater-coaching/. Subscribe to my newsletter 'Purpose With Myriem' and join a community of like-minded professionals who are also on a journey to discover and live their purpose. I regularly share tips, insights and success stories that could be just the inspiration you need.

**The 'PurposeCast' podcast**: Tune into my podcast, Purpose-Cast, on Spotify or Apple Podcasts, where I dive deep into topics related to career change, personal growth and living a purpose-driven life. Each episode features insights, inter-views and actionable advice to help you on your journey.

**Online courses**: I offer a range of online courses designed to help you deepen your understanding of purpose, vision, career change and mindset. These courses provide practi-cal tools and strategies to guide you through every step of your journey. Whether you're looking to clarify your vision, shift your mindset, or take actionable steps towards a career change, there's a course tailored to your needs.

Visit Purposeek Online Courses at purposeekcoaching.com. au/career-change-coaching-online-courses/ to learn more and enrol today.

# About
# the Author

MYRIEM SLATER was born in Casablanca, Morocco, and her journey has since taken her across the globe. After completing business studies in France, she embarked on a career in finance consulting, working in France before moving to Sydney, Australia in 2010, which she now calls home.

Over fifteen years as a finance consultant, Myriem climbed the corporate ladder and mastered the demands of the industry. However, despite her success, she always felt a deep sense of dissatisfaction. Though she appreciated the challenges that came with the role, she knew something was missing. Ultimately, the signs of burnout became impossible to ignore, and the joy she once found in her work disappeared.

This realisation led Myriem to take a bold leap by pausing her career and embarking on a personal and career development journey that transformed her life. Through deep introspection, she began exploring the concept of 'purpose', questioning her own and searching for a path that aligned with her true self. This journey unlocked new doors for her and allowed her to realign with her passions and true identity.

Today, Myriem is an entrepreneur and career coach, helping others find their purpose and true career path through the Purposeek Coaching Method, a method born from her own experiences of career change and self-discovery. Her mission is to guide others through their own transitions and empower them to lead purpose-driven lives.

Myriem is also the host of PurposeCast, a podcast where she explores topics related to purpose, personal growth and career transitions, offering insights and interviews to inspire listeners on their own journeys.

Becoming an author was one of Myriem's lifelong dreams, and she is thrilled to have fulfilled that dream with the publication of her first book, *Career Change is Chaos... Unless You Find Your Purple Purpose.* She is excited to continue sharing her knowledge and experiences through future books, with the hope of inspiring others to pursue their own purpose-driven journeys.